JEFF TOVAR

SUCCESS LEAVES CLUES

Tips that worked for me

With Milana L. Walter

Success Leaves Clues
Copyright © 2014 by Jeff Tovar

Published by:
Dunamis Woman Media & Publishing
P.O. Box 59676
Schaumburg, IL 60159

Contact Us:
publisher@dunamis-woman.com
847.908.0650

ISBN 978-0-9860248-1-8

Book design and production at
OneTouchPoint/Ginny's Printing
Austin, Texas

Printed in the United States of America

TABLE OF CONTENTS

Acknowledgements

THANK YOU TO SO MANY

Especially my parents—You have given me many gifts. I know I can never repay them all. I will try and pay them forward.

To my sister—You always ask me about business....well here it is!

And to the two most amazing people I know my daughters Kyla and Brenna. You are amazing students, athletes and people. I want only the best for you.

I LOVE YOU ALL

— *Jeff*

WHY

I have had help from many writing this book and if you read it, you will see I have help in all areas of my life. A friend of mine once said, "I am not sure if you can do anything, everything is done for you." A special thanks to Kathy Passarelli and Milana Walter; you both did so much (I am pretty sure my mom and Kathy are the only people on the planet that can read my writing).

Why did I write this book? I wrote it for my two daughters hoping that something in here is useful for them. They have had some good times and some bad times in their young lives. If they someday read this book and realize that life is what you make it so start to make it great today, find great teachers and only learn from the best, that happiness comes from within, conquer your fear and take big chances. You have nothing to lose and make learning and change a part of their lives, and then I will have succeeded.

I have written for all the Tovar Heroes who work incredibly long hours in the winter, do whatever it takes, and who truly make the impossible possible. These snow warriors truly battle Mother Nature to ease the stress of our customers and their customer's lives on days that the world would have been shut down 30 years ago (at least the piece of the world we know).

And, I have written this for anyone who wants to achieve something more. Whatever 'more' is for you. If this book helps one person in some way, I will have succeeded.

"You have to count your little wins."

— *Bernard Rollin*

I Play to Win!!

Clear your mind of "CAN'T." Don't let yourself think, "No I can't, I am not good enough." Champions are not born, they are made. In order to be successful, you have to be relentless about continuous improvement. This is one of my dad's common pep talks to me and my sister. In order to do great things you have to dream big and work hard to achieve your goals. Trust me, winning does not come easy.

He also teaches us that at the same time you have to keep things fun. Celebrate the little victories because the little victories build to the big victories.

Sometimes you have to take charge. I was appointed co-captain to my soccer team and this is an important job to me. It is not about me winning, it is about my team winning. This means I have to be a leader, not a boss. I work with my team and point out all the good things they do so we can keep progressing.

There will be a time for beat downs or talking about what we can do better. However, beat downs shall not be part of your everyday routine. I believe focusing on our positives gives us a better result, especially at game time.

These are some things that my dad has taught me. Now it is your turn! Wake up each day with determination and go to bed with satisfaction. GAME ON!!

— *Brenna Tovar*

"Don't look back leave it all on the track."

— *Racing Stripes, 2005*

Life's Not Fair

I hear this up to fifty times a day from my dad, Jeff Tovar. Jeff Tovar is not only a wonderful father, he is a mentor, and is the CEO and President of Tovar Snow Professionals. Throughout high school and college he would mow lawns even though he had the dream of being a veterinarian. While pursuing his degree, his professor asked him to write a business plan about his lawn maintenance company. He then realized that he did not want to be a veterinarian and he was going to turn his business plan that he wrote into a real business. It was not an easy task. When he first got out of college, he lived in his shop with huge rats everywhere, so he could save money for his company. Now, here he is about 25 years later, with a company that went from approximately ten trucks to thousands of trucks. He got there with the help from mentors that would tell him lessons they used to be successful.

The unique thing about my family is that we are all crazy competitive and like to be uncomfortable. I ride horses and I remember when I first started riding, jumped about eighteen inches in my first show. I did great at it; however my dad wanted me to move up. He and my trainer both believed in me, so he helped me to move up to a class that was 2'6 feet. To say I was crazy nervous would have been an understatement. But I practiced and my dad gave me little pep talks all the time. Now two years later, because I was uncomfortable and got pushed to get out of my comfort zone to do it, I have been to Nationals and hoping to go to the North American Young Riders Championships in about two years.

Since I was little, my dad helped my sister and me to believe that we could be something great. However, my dad believes that if you don't push yourself and make yourself get nervous you can't advance. Furthermore, you also need the help from people that have already been in your position. My dad uses mentors and takes the big picture of what they tell him and applies it to his own life. Now it is your turn to take all of the lessons that my dad and many other successful people have used, and place it in your life.

— *Kyla Tovar*

We All Have Issues, Problems & Sins

"Nothing in this world can take the place of persistence...Persistence and determination alone are omnipotent."

— *Calvin Coolidge*

If you are breathing, you have issues; if you are alive, you are going to have some problems. As Jesus Christ said, "He who is without sin may cast the first stone." We are all human doing the best we know to do at the time: meandering through this thing called life and issues, problems and sins come with the territory. I always say that no one has more issues than me except one of my best friends, Steve Fuzinski. Steve is proud to say no one has more issues than him. He is a self—made guy. Steve owns a snowplow business and in order to do that you have to be a little off. Steve is also a multi—millionaire and living a wonderful life even with his issues.

Where does he put his energy? Definitely NOT in worrying about his issues. Steve focuses his energy to work through them and on them and most importantly, he works to his strengths. Because of this, he is very successful by his own definition of success. You don't have to be great at everything to have a wonderful life and career, just be great at one thing. If you can figure out what you are good at and then become great at it and love what you do, you are destined to live a wonderful life.

Easier said than done? Not if you start by asking yourself these questions, "What is it I love to do? How can I build a career around it?" The next step would be to find others who do what you love, are already successful, and learn the steps they took.

First, realize there are no "have to's" in this life; only "get to's." There is no definition of what success looks like for you except the one you create. Your success is custom-made. Success does leave clues. Take some time and figure out what success would look like for you and really examine it. Is it about a career? A certain amount of money? Being a great father? Or, the best NFL running back?

Once you have a solid clue as to what success means for you, I hope that in sharing what worked and works for me in my journey may equip you with some tools and clues to get from where you are to where you want to be. Once you decide where you want to be, success is a step-by-step process. Don't think success will only happen when you reach a certain point, location or destination. You've heard it many times I'm sure—life is about the journey, not necessarily about the destination. I find this to be absolutely true.

Enjoy the journey. Inside the journey lie the story, your story, lessons, and epiphanies. Because it is during the journey where most of your time and energy will be spent; do not put your life on hold. In each day, there is something relevant to learn. Don't put off today what you probably should have done yesterday! Dr. Bernard Rollin, one of my mentors, would always say, "You have to celebrate your little victories every day."

Many times our parents, teachers or whomever try to save us from the pain and disappointment of some life lesson yet to be learned. Often, we go forward and do whatever—the way we want to do it. Sometimes, doing it our way and failing to listen is the way we learn the lesson. We had to see for ourselves. No one could tell us or protect us from the life stuff. There comes a time when we have to get over ourselves (get out of our own way) to take the easy way instead of thinking it doesn't count as our victory if we use the advice from someone else.

This book will tell stories about mentors. It is about what has worked for me in my journey of success. I am not perfect, but I love what I do every day about 90% of the time. If I have a complaint at all, it is that I wish I had more time to enjoy the many good things in my life. Overall, I am blessed to live a wonderful life and have two incredible daughters who are great students and excel in their afterschool activities. I run a business, which does well because of a team of great people that I call "Tovar Heroes." I am fortunate enough to spend my days with them. I take time for my friends and family throughout the year and get to do fantastic things in great places all over the planet.

This book is based on what I call, The Tovar Way. The Tovar Way works for me and has given me great success according to what I feel success is for me. You have to decide what success is to you. Use this book to assist you in obtaining everything in your life that defines success. On the other hand, allow it to help recognize and discard the things that hinder you from being who you truly are in your world and for the world at large.

However, understand you can't get there unless you decide where you want to go. If you want to take a vacation, you have to know where you want to go, right? Planning a vacation to Mexico takes a different kind of planning than a trip to Australia. Visualize your goal and "see it, imagine it." You're going to be constantly off course but you have to be persistent.

Think of Captain Jim Lovell, the astronaut played by Tom Hanks in the movie, Apollo 13. He said, "From now on, we live in a world where man has walked on the moon. And, it's not a miracle, we just decide to go."

I say that to you just decide where you want to go in your life. Period.

The Tovar Way describes the values, beliefs, principles and practices that are the foundation of our unique culture and our unique way at our company, Tovar Snow Professionals. We are a company that provides snow plowing and chemical services for commercial customers in Illinois, northwest Indiana and southern Wisconsin. The Tovar Way explains how we relate to each other, our customers and even our vendors. It is who we are and it is what drives our extraordinary success.

Now this did not come about overnight; it came about over a lifetime. However, the actual document took about a year to write. As I often do, I found a mentor, David Friedman, who had done this and had great success at his company and I had him show me the way. This is why it is done quickly and well. I found an expert, asked for help and followed his guidance.

These Fundamentals are a guidebook for over 3,000+ employees for making decisions on the job. This empowers our team to do the right thing for the right reasons and without slowing down wondering what to do or waiting for a supervisor to make every decision. The fundamentals provide a blueprint to success at our company.

THE TOVAR WAY FUNDAMENTALS ARE:

- Deliver heroic customer service
- Be passionate about quality
- Always do the right thing
- Check the ego at the door
- Take responsibility for achieving results
- Be relentless about continuous improvement
- Be a team player
- Practice blameless problem-solving
- Always think big
- Work with a sense of urgency to get things done
- Face challenges head-on and find solutions
- Be a rock that others can count on
- Look for the positive
- Listen generously
- Speak straight
- Honor commitments
- Be for each other
- Regularly provide meaningful acknowledgement and appreciation
- Set and ask for expectations
- Embrace change
- Conquer your fear
- Keep things fun

Furthermore, I believe these fundamentals and ideas can help each of us in life. I believe that this book, like many things, has some great ideas. So try it, see if there are a few ideas in here that can help you make your life all you want it to be.

Remember, success leaves clues. I hope there are one or two clues to guide you to your success.

Always Do the Right Thing and Keep Things Fun

"Choose a job you love, and you will never have
to work a day in your life."

— *Confucius*

Are you trying to do everything on your own? Do you shy away from asking for help? Well, how is that working for you?

Starting with my Dad and his 3-D's—Drive, Desire and Determination—I learned to ask and listen. I am not going to say it has been easy; but I have been able to follow steps taken by the right mentors for me, and replicate their success. I have no secrets to success. I know what worked for me, and I want to share this information and my experiences with you in hopes of making a positive difference in your life.

Our work—whether you are in the snow business like me or a teacher, nurse, paramedic—it is a vital part of our lives, it is through our work that we serve humanity, and in many ways discover our true purpose in life. I believe this to be true whether we own a business or work for one. The way Oswald Spengler, a German philosopher, expresses this point resonates with me. He says, "This is our purpose: to make as meaningful as possible this life that has been bestowed upon us, to live in such a way that we may be proud of ourselves, to act in such a way that some part of us lives on."

As mentioned previously, the following chapters are the *Tovar Way*. The *Tovar Way* is comprised of 22 fundamentals which "describe the values, behaviors, principles, and practices that are the foundation of our unique culture. It explains how we relate to each other, our customers, and even our vendors. It's who we are and what drives our extraordinary success." These guidelines were born out of the reality that we had to do something different if we wanted Tovar Snow Professionals (TSP) to thrive in the business game and fund our charity, Snow Angels (formerly "Tovar Cares").

A few years back—after being away for a while because of an injury from a snowmobile accident—TSP had developed some cultural issues. There were some employees with pretty bad attitudes and we knew what we had to do. We had not terminated anyone for a few years, even when we should have. Why? Because firing people is difficult to do. One of my chief duties in the company is to hold people accountable and more often than not, that means having to do unpleasant and uncomfortable tasks for the overall good of TSP.

The question facing us–facing me-what do we do to make the working environment healthy again? Step one was to offer fifteen employees the 'opportunity' to continue their careers somewhere else.

We had allowed people to stay on even after they had already checked-out mentally. Why did we do this? Because as I said, it is hard to fire people or because they had been with us awhile and we gave them the chance to come back around. However, they did not. *They were poison* and by allowing the poison to stay, we were forcing our good people to drink it and be affected by their toxicity every workday.

Often, a major stumbling block to success is the avoidance of doing things such as terminating someone because it is uncomfortable.

Step two was to create a strong company culture based on 22 solid fundamentals. I hired a friend and mentor, David Friedman, from Vistage, the world's leading Chief Executive Officer Organization, who did this at his own company. He came in and helped me to develop the *Tovar Way*, 22 fundamentals. Then, we rolled them out to the TSP team by conducting a series of meetings to teach the fundamentals and continued to integrate them in our culture on a weekly basis.

Even today, our meetings begin with talking about the weeks' fundamental and we rotate one employee per week to write about that week's *Tovar Way*. We are always seeking new ways to share and teach these fundamentals.

TOVAR WAY FUNDAMENTAL: ALWAYS DO THE RIGHT THING

Fun and integrity, a mismatch? Hardly. Compatible in the sense of authenticity, they are actually kindred spirits.

If you always do the right thing, you will not have to lie. Integrity is a personal choice. It is not about convenience it is about personal standards. What is doing the right thing? Is it naïve to think that doing the right thing is always so crystal clear or can doing the right thing not be so clear at all?

Surprisingly, a Spike Lee movie, "*Do the Right Thing*" comes to mind. I think I was still in college when it came out. The story rolls out on one of the hottest summer days of the year in Brooklyn's Bed Stuyvesant, a multi-cultural working class neighborhood where most did not have the benefit of air conditioning. Tempers flared as the heat turned into sweat, turned up the volume on latent racial overtones, exclusionary traditions, and seething anger between neighbors. Each neighbor thought their way was the right way and the others were wrong. The film portrayed a dramatic lesson on clear and blurred lines drawn as each one insisted their way was the way to do the right thing.

I have heard people say you cannot get ahead if you do the right thing. They believe people who succeed have compromised their values and are liars, cheaters and thieves. That may be true sometimes; I am not going to tell you there are not any bad people in the world. Bad things do happen. Bad people do exist.

We all have to define our own right and wrong. I believe that by doing the right thing, it will come back to you. I also believe that at least 98% of the world's population is made up of good people. Unfortunately, the scumbags of the world dominate the fear-focused news. There are loads of great people who have tremendous success in business and in life.

In her book, *Doing the Right Thing for the Right Reasons*, Barbara Killinger, PhD defines integrity as "…an uncompromising predictably, consistent commitment to honor moral, ethical, spiritual and artistic values and principles."

Integrity is a main ingredient of the heart and soul of a person as well as an organization. We see it as an unwavering commitment to do the right thing in every circumstance, every time. Ask yourself, "Will I be proud of what I am about to do?" Will it be the right thing for the customer, for the company and right for you? We take a long-term view of success, making decisions that build strong trusting relationships. Trust in fact, takes years to build, but can be lost in an instant with a blatant lie. Warren Buffet said it right, "It takes 20 years to build a reputation and five minutes to ruin it. If you think about that you'll do things differently."

Former President Richard Nixon, Lance Armstrong and Bernie Madoff are known more for their lies than their accomplishments. We earn people's trust by demonstrating integrity in every action we take and in every decision we make.

I always want to do the right thing. Less than honorable people have burned me sometimes. When you are betrayed or lied to, it makes you want to say the heck with people why do the right thing? Why do positive things? I may be burned again, but in the end, my life is good. I refuse to allow a few rotten people to sour me on everyone else.

Let me tell you what happened when I met the owner of GTL, GreenTree Landscape (name changed for confidentiality). I was in my twenties and was on a tour with ILCA, Illinois Landscape Contractors Association. I came to meet the owner and tour this very impressive landscape company. Just to put it in perspective: I had five trucks, they had 50. Like many landscape businesses, it is family-owned, and the father is the founder and CEO, his son and daughter run the day-to-day operation. The other contractors and I were guided to the conference room after touring the massive facility. Then the owner lit into us! "**You all** are destroying the landscape business with your under pricing and the way you prune the bushes!" Now, I'll admit, he was not exactly wrong but his personal attack against us was loaded with bitterness; and was so nasty. After that attack, his kids spoke in an upbeat and mostly positive matter. They were very proud of what their father had achieved with GTL, as they should have been. But this guy would burn us on the business and he was a negative force. I knew indirectly he was a mentor of how not to be. I left that situation, clear in the knowledge, "I NEVER want to be like that guy!" He blamed other people for his problems.

Some years later, the U.S. economy went into crisis mode. We almost fell into a massive depression. We hit a tough spot at TSP. I felt like everything I had learned was wrong. So did some of my fellow business owners. I even had a 'poor me' moment but I had to get over that quickly. I looked for mentors who had experienced something like this before. There weren't many still alive who experienced the Great Depression. This economic crisis was unprecedented in this time and place. I had to try new things and experiment. Our business fundamentals did not change but we had to be more nimble. We had to learn how to press the reset button; and that is what we did to recover.

TOVAR WAY FUNDAMENTAL: KEEP THINGS FUN

The idea was to do what you love and you will have great success. For me, creating a business was fun and although how I did it in my 20s is different from how I do it in my 40s, it has always been fun.

What's not to have fun about?! My team and I are snow people, plain and simple, and snow is *fun*. Well, for our crew anyway. It is important to love what you do and as the saying goes, "you will never work a day in your life if you do what you love."

Though we approach our jobs with passion and commitment, especially in our crazy season, we do not take ourselves too seriously. Fun, laughter and play help us keep perspective, renew our spirit and stay energized.

Fun in action triggers right brain creativity that inspires a competitive edge. The visionaries who lead Apple, Google and Nike have created sprawling campus environments as workspaces and a supportive attitude for play that lend greatly to their competitive edge. The combination of work and play engages employees, induces innovation and creativity and reduces stress. TSP has a pontoon boat we use for team building on the water. When TSP takes to the water, we expect each team to do their weekly meetings on the pontoon boat and cruise the river for an early dinner. Mixing work and play, builds the team and keeps things fun.

We also seek out beautiful surroundings to hold mini-motivational retreats and company picnics. We even have softball and bowling teams, as well as four-day workweeks in May and June. In addition,

TSP has a company condominium at Lake Geneva for employees and their families to enjoy a weekend on TSP.

We work our tails off during the snow season and it is important that they know how much they are valued and appreciated.

Scientific studies support that people in a positive, happy state of mind increases productivity by 50%. Being in a state of fun takes the pressure off, stretches one memory, sharpens senses, transform awareness, increases engagement by creating emotions and focus ability around play. Fun and play encourages remembering favorable moments and challenges that stimulates our ability that many times create social bonds, communication and experiences.

The residue of fun can endure over time. We learn self-awareness through fun and play.

Plato said, "You can discover more about a person in an hour of play than in a year of conversation."

Fun nurtures the liberation of one's spirit. Believe it, or not, having fun is the right thing to do. Because I like sports, played sports throughout college, and continue to be an ardent spectator, I understand the benefit of play. However, do not get it twisted; having fun is not synonymous with cluelessness and irresponsibility.

I believe you get what you focus on. Fun is a choice. Happiness is a choice. We all have good luck. We all have bad luck. If you focus on the bad, you attract more bad. If you focus on the good, you attract more good. At the start of each day, I get up and take five minutes to express my gratitude for all the good things in my life. It is my choice to be grateful and happy instead of the opposite.

I live with an 'attitude of gratitude.' You cannot be happy until you are grateful for all of the good—and even the bad—in your life. Here is something I hold to be true that we are not taught as children (or adults): You can determine how happy you are. Your happiness is between your ears. Decide to be happy and you will be. Decide to have fun and you will.

Living in this vain is a choice. We choose the effects of things in our lives. It is not so much what happens to us but how we respond to what happens to us that determines our outlook on life, and our outcomes.

Do you really have a choice to be happy or miserable? I believe we do but of course, there are a few exceptions.

Some people are always happy; some are always miserable. Do you really think everything goes perfect for those who are happy? No. *They decide* to be happy. They have *made a choice* between being happy or miserable. They chose *happy*. You can be happy and have fun in almost every moment of your life. Your attitude determines your altitude, and how you see life.

ARE YOU OPEN OR STUCK?

In the book, "The Luck Factor: Changing Your Luck, Changing Your Life with Four Essential Principles" by Richard Wiseman, Head of Psychology Research at University of Hertfordshire in England, is the study of one principle that fascinates me. Wiseman's study concludes that good luck odds are improved when you turn bad luck into good by seeing how you can make lemonade out of lemons. He further says, "Lucky people are open to new experiences. Unlucky people are stuck in routines." (From an article in Fast Company by Daniel H. Pink)

"Most folks are as happy as they make up their minds to be."

— *Abe Lincoln*

Conquer Fear and Embrace Change

"The only thing to fear is fear itself."

— President Franklin Delano Roosevelt

Do you fear the worst when you step out of your comfort zone? We all have fears but if you will allow yourself to see the fear factor for what it really is—**F**alse **E**vidence **A**ppearing **R**eal— then intimidation diminishes and fear subsides. I believe too often, we beat ourselves down with worry; and sweating the notion that when good things happen, we can expect bad things to follow. If and when bad things do happen, do what I do, deal with them immediately.

Do not get the impression that I am immune to fear. Hardly. However, I have learned I have a choice: be consumed or be in control. I would not own a multi-million dollar business waddling neck-deep in the hell of fear. I say, when you're driving through hell, drive faster! Hurry up and get the **hell of fear** out of your system: your heart, mind, body and spirit.

Put the hell behind you and get back to all the good that life has to offer. You say, easier said than done, right?

It takes strength to conquer fear and embrace change. Some of us can conjure up strength on our own without support from others, however many of us need assistance. All of us need to believe that positive outcomes are not pipe dreams but are truly real.

Positive outcomes stem from paying attention to the details of a matter and then working to pursue and prepare a solution. Positive outcomes stem from movement versus being stuck in fear. Talk your fear through with someone whose opinion you respect: whether a professional or personal contact. However, be cautious not to share names or any other specific information that would compromise privacy or confidentiality. To conquer fear one has to take a stand that may feel scary or uncomfortable initially. I find the more information I collect about things that create fear, the more comfortable and confident I become. I know I have done my troubleshooting or problem-solving homework. Preparation is essential to building the strength to conquer fear and embrace change.

Want to know my main tool for preparation in conquering fear, embracing change and just living life? I got a BHAG: Big Hairy Audacious Goal! read it in "Built to Last." This book encourages making your own BHAGS, goals that are seemingly too big for you. Well BHAGS **stuck** with me. Creating your own path helps to diminish the fear of the unknown. So make realistic goals but not easy ones, you want to make goals that stretch you and help you overcome your fears.

A physical and mental connection happens when we write down our thoughts. It is scientifically proven, not something I made up. The preparation in writing down goals has been very powerful for me. I attribute much of my success to goal setting. Even now, I continue to refine what works for me and add new BHAGS each year. For the most part, the system outlined by Tony Robbins in his book, *Awaken the Giant*, works for me. I am not going to get into Robbins' system in great depth, but I will share the basic premise. Tony talks about contemplating and setting goals in four areas of life: 1) Personal development, 2) Career and money, 3) Toys and adventure and 4) Contribution.

I have followed this program since 2000, the launch of the New Millennium. What is amazing is that almost *all the goals I set my sights on I achieved. I kid you not.* I wrote down goals that led to purchasing a condo for my parents near my home when they would come visit me and their granddaughters; to grow my company the right way; and to meet the right mentors to help me shape what Tovar is today. I also set and met a goal to find the right property at the right price for the mentoring camp, "Snow Angels." In addition to writing goals down, there has to be 'action' applied. Such as a photo in clear sight of a property I envisioned for the camp; a condo that resembled the one I wanted and envisioned an article about the company in a magazine like Forbes but attaching a picture of our office building on the cover of Forbes.

There is still one goal I have yet to conquer: losing a few pounds! Seems strange how hard that is to achieve but I believe I will. I still keep my notes from 2000 with my goals checked off in my Day Planner. There is great power when goals are committed to writing, reviewed frequently and activated. The conscious pursuit of something such as looking for that new home you want or educational opportunities or a dream vacation you want to take is necessary. You have to put your energy into them—not just think, sit and do nothing. Focus is a key component. So prioritize: maybe set no more than 5 goals at a time. Focus on those only so you do not spread yourself thin. In my opinion, too few people take the time to write goals and it is not hard to do. It takes me on an average three hours per year to write them down and a few minutes each week to review them!

Goal setting may help overcome fear. Start with small goals. Once you achieve a goal then you begin to conquer your fear of failure. Each July, I revisit my goals and rewrite them for the next year; and then for the next three, five, 10, or 20 years, whatever feels right for me. I always have a goal for each of the four categories for the current year. Then, if needed, write some longer-term goals. Remember it is all up to you: your goals are yours, not anyone else's.

I then review my goals each month and put action behind them. Action. Action. Action. Back when I wanted the property for Snow Angels, I updated the generic photo of a property, started looking at properties and picked up real estate brochures/sheets with more specifics on the type of property I was looking for. Then I placed the real estate brochure/sheet for the property in plain sight where I could eyeball it often. I then updated my goals and knew, "*I will get this property or something better.*" Someone else out-bid me on a property I thought was perfect. For a minute, I could not understand it. However, I kept positive and a much better property at a much better price came along. Keep believing and know something better is on the way.

Imagine. Allow yourself to really "see" yourself. Goal setting is personal, actually fun, easy and a tried and true tool for manifestation. It is just as easy to take a few steps and have positive outcomes. Sadly, most people do what other people do or think instead of following what feels right for them. It takes strength and someone sharing information. Since success leaves clues, I want to share four steps to jump-start your path to successful goal setting and personal and professional expectations:

Step 1: Decide where you want to go
Step 2: Find a mentor and create a plan (and read about those who have done it before)
Step 3: Follow the plan and the advice given by the mentor.
Step 4: Adjust and persevere until you achieve your goal.

TOVAR WAY FUNDAMENTAL: CONQUER FEAR

Give yourself permission to dream and think big. Thinking big embraces change and requires you to step out of making decisions based on fear. Sometimes, it means letting go of what we know to be safe and secure and walking away from what is familiar in order to become the best that we can be. Growth never happens without taking calculated risks. Be willing to face your fears and accomplish great things that fit you in spite of them. Do not let the hell of fear keep you from the heaven of big dreams.

You cannot win big if you fear winning. When I was a kid mowing lawns, I always knew there would be a day when I would have hundreds of crews. I kept this dream to myself but I somehow knew. Now my crews are in the thousands and instead of landscape and lawns, they are snow and ice management crews.

Things did not always go the way I planned. I had to make some changes. I had no problem being in the landscape business that also plowed snow. However, when I chose to focus exclusively on snow plowing, the company grew faster than it would have doing both landscaping and snow.

We thrive on the thrill of the snow. Every snow event feels like an adrenaline-pumping fire drill, all hands on deck, jumping into the caravan of massive snowplow trucks veering off in different directions to clear the snow so TSP customers can walk, drive and park in a safe environment. *What a rush*!

Fear can also be a rush, but in most cases, fear is an energy drain. Fear freezes growth and change. Living with fear attracts other negative emotions such as anger, aggression and jealousy. We can get very cozy with dysfunction and negativity to a point that the thought and action of the pursuit of a possible better way becomes frozen in fear. We can rationalize that because the dysfunction is familiar and we have adapted to coping skills to tolerate versus venturing out into the wild, Wild West of the unfamiliar but potentially happier life.

A TSP employee recants how fear was a draining factor in their work environment and how mentoring sessions with Coach Giselle Chapman, a chief creative optimizer, presented a different perspective.

> *"I began working with Giselle because of an issue I was having with a co-worker. I was convinced that person wanted me fired. The first time Giselle and I sat down, I began telling her about the issue and trying to prove to her, I was right. After everything was out, she asked, 'how are you going to solve your problem?' I couldn't believe it. I just spent 30 minutes pointing out my co-worker's problems and Giselle couldn't see them! I started defending myself and showing Giselle how it wasn't me, it was my co-worker: they did this, they did that, and they don't care. On and on I went.*
>
> *Giselle told me even if all that was true I was the one that felt that way: I was the one worrying, afraid of the co-worker trying to get me fired. They may be all these things that I said they were **but I am the one** feeling this way.*
>
> *To hear and accept that was a tough pill to swallow. Here I thought I was going to be validated for my feelings and I got exactly the opposite. At this point, my comfort level was zero and my fear was greater than ever. Now she was on their side too (in my mind) and I was outnumbered. Giselle and I continued to work together once a month over the next year and the more we spoke the more I saw what she was saying and why she was right.*
>
> *Fear was my problem. I created it. Even if my co-worker was all those things I believed, I was the one choosing to let it*

affect me, which was bringing down my performance in the company. I started to learn that I had my own part to play in the relationship and I wasn't doing anything to help it.

Before my work with Giselle, I believed that if I moved past all my reasons and tried to mend the relationship, I was excusing the behavior of my co-worker. I couldn't have been more wrong. Giselle taught me to own my piece, whatever it may be. I learned to conquer my fear of them, their actions, and their behavior by doing everything I could to fix my behavior.

None of this fixes the relationship and through all of it, I learned that isn't within anybody's power to do. All I can do is fix myself and keep fear at bay. My job is to make sure I am the best me I can be, hoping the other person is doing the same. If both people can focus on that the relationship will fix itself."

It takes strength to conquer fear. George Lucas' Star Wars trilogy, the seeming fearlessness of the Jedi is based on the belief of a powerful, positive energy within them called "The Force." They chose to believe in the reality of a positive powerful energy. Yoda said, "Fear is the path to the dark." What is your "Force?"

One thing we can control is our actions and how we respond to life stuff. We know dark sides exist but do we chose to dwell on them and be sucked in by them? Or do we choose the side where we build faith in the positive, gain insight and strength, focus on what's happening NOW and seek out where we feel celebrated instead of tolerated?

Sometimes the risk lies in not taking the risk. And what is usually the source of indecision which stops progress? Fear. Fear freezes action. We have to be strong enough to press forward through the barriers. "The journey of a thousand miles begins with one step"; "You cannot make it to 2nd base with both feet on first." "The only thing to fear is fear itself." Does fear have you frozen from moving forward? If you allow fear to overtake you, you have to conquer your fear and work through it to achieve your goal. Battle fear with strength and conviction, do not take no for an answer; continue to execute the plan your gut, wisdom, or intuition supports. Wisdom usually whispers, ego mostly yells.

A small case of the jitters can be a positive thing as long as you do not shut down from fear and forward action.

I know you've heard the saying by Frederick Nietzsche in recent songs, "What doesn't kill you makes you stronger."

What did I fear when I thought I was about to go out of business? I fought fear and instead sought wisdom from a mentor who had been where I was. What did he do? Our situations were not exact, but it was an approach to this kind of problem, and solution that I was seeking.

I am persistent. I will persevere. I do my homework. I do not have a fear of losing material stuff. My happiness does not come from owning stuff. It is not about ego. I just believe that if I put my heart and soul into something and follow my gut, I can overcome any obstacle. I am not just taking a risk. I am taking a calculated risk.

When the curtain was pulled back on America's financial health during the 2008-2010 Economic Crisis, we saw the credit system models instituted after World War II exposed for what they had morphed to be: enticing vehicles that indebted people with items they could not afford. The buy now, pay later credit system had created a false sense of wealth as opposed to the original intent of saving cash flow by buying on time and lay-away.

The American Dream was compromised—again—in a way most did not think possible.

When I started my business, I reinvested 80% of the profits. I had no risk. I had nothing to lose. In college, I was the guy who lived in the 'manure-house', worse than the movie, *Animal House*. It was the party house. Every week windows would get broken: like clockwork. It was one of the best times in my young life.

So fast forward to after I graduated from Colorado State and came back to Illinois. It was a no-brainer when my dog, Zeus, and I lived in my shop for a year. I was a single guy and my goals were set on saving money and taking my landscape business to another level.

But living at the shop had its moments: I had a feeling Zeus and I were not alone. My friend and business partner, Steve and I go back to our early school years and have many shared experiences. I told

Steve there was a lot of scratching in the walls at night and I thought it might be mice. Then one night, Steve and I had a stare-down with a super-rat in the shop: literally eyeball-to-eyeball. We kept our eyes planted on this creature, stayed still and then figured we needed to calmly get moving before the rat got agitated with us. It was then confirmed; my shop/home had a mega rat problem.

Today, I reinvest 75% of every dollar made and I live in a nice house with my daughters, without a super-rat in sight.

I believe in the power of positive thinking and I do not allow naysayers to penetrate or alter my thoughts. I am not afraid to work nor am I ashamed or embarrassed if I would have to deliver pizzas in order to keep a roof over my family's head. However, my thoughts about pizzerias would not be only as a delivery guy. I would be thinking, "How do I own one of these places?" It is how I think…and by the way, the pizza shop would be in the Bahamas.

TOVAR WAY FUNDAMENTAL: EMBRACE CHANGE

Many people avoid change.

"I hate change," a friend and competitor once said to me. He asked, "How do you grow your business so fast and have such great profits? I have been doing this for years and cannot figure it out." I said, "We adapt and we change quickly." He said, "I hate change."

Nothing ever stays the same, thankfully. Change creates energy and excitement. Be inspired by both the challenges and the possibilities that change brings. In business, we need to change faster internally than the marketplace changes externally. The better and faster we are in adapting to change, the stronger and more successful we become as a company.

Jack Welch, former chairman of GE, has a couple of quotes I like on "change:" "Willingness to change is a strength…" and "If the change outside your company is happening faster than the change inside, the end is near."

Then there is change that most did not anticipate like the economic crisis. Even a daring, self-made multi-millionaire like Steve Fuzinski, CEO of Green Sweep Inc., reflects on how he was blind-sided, tested and shaken from the core, *"Everything we had known before was over. We had such a radical change. Right before our eyes, our world changed so fast and we finally had to change if we were going to succeed. I didn't like the change at first. Pricing went down 30-40% in one year. No one I knew had 40% margins in the first place. To make it, we had to become super-super lean. Our customers owned real estate so they had to adapt to the drastic change by cutting things like crazy, including the fees for snow removal service, but still wanted the same or even better service. You do not need a license to be a snow removal company.*

Our customers were forced to give unqualified vendors a shot for the sake of saving money. Any guy with a snowplow truck was considered. Earnings from snow removal were named 'blood money' because the work and demands were so terrible.

This is the only business I know where you push all your chips in the middle of the table and then bet. In our business, we don't make any money for eight months out of twelve. That is why, to be in this business, one has to be a great banker. You have to be on top of your finances."

The act of putting yourself out there terrorizes many people: like being stripped butt-naked in front of a crowd without your consent. Take those brave entrepreneurs who willingly appear before an audience of millions on the TV show, *Shark Tank*. Outside of the U.S. the show was called, *Dragon's Den*. These entrepreneurs lay their fears aside for the opportunity to secure a "Shark"—potential multi-millionaire and billionaire investors—with millions of critical eyes watching. They go there with a goal, to leave *Shark Tank* with a deal in hand. Although to pursue change can be scary; running a business from payment to payment, or being properly supported with the necessary financial, technical, mentoring support is well worth a slight case of temporary anxiety.

When Tovar changed to a snow-only company, it was not a big deal to our team and me because we had done our due diligence. Many others thought we had gone crazy! Yes, it was a huge change and a bold move no matter how justified. One thing for sure, because many people resist change, an impending change really shakes people up.

Early on in my college education, Professor Bernard Rollin at Colorado State University challenged the way I thought about my role in the study of animal science. On the path to become a DVM, though my connection to animals was special, I realized that owning a business was better suited for me. The landscape business I had started as a kid, continued to flourish while I was away in Colorado thanks to help from my dad and sister. I also knew that being successful in business would allow me to be an advocate and a philanthropist for humans and animals. The philosophy class taught by Professor Rollin, which continues to be game changing for me, inspired me.

The epiphany came when I realized my initial goal of becoming a DVM and establishing a chain of animal clinics had changed. My advisor, the late Dr. Ed Pexton, I have to thank for leaving the clues of his knowledge and success by pointing me in the direction to study business and build on the fact I was already a business owner. My senior year, he asked me to write a business plan (which I earned 12 college credits for doing). Creating that business plan, opened my mind and helped me to organize my thoughts and see costs and revenue from a more informed perspective. Then Dr. Pexton introduced me to Dr. Velk, a professor in the business department and more clues came together because the next thing I knew, I now had a name for what I did—*entrepreneur*. I was a bona-fide entrepreneur.

Change.... What would not have happened had I resisted it? Never looked back. Motivational Powerhouse and author Wayne Dyer said, "When you change the way you look at things, the things you look at change."

Understand, you can never change the ways of other people but you can change your ways.

"I'm starting with the man (woman) in the mirror. I am asking him (her) to change his (her) ways and no message could have been clearer, if you want to make the world a better place, take a look at yourself and make that change." ("Man in the Mirror" by Michael Jackson)

First, we have to look at ourselves to make the change inside us if we want to see change on the outside.

On the CBS Evening News, a study cited responses from one hundred 85-year-old men and women who were asked, "If in your life, you could have done something different, what would it be? The overwhelming response, "I would have taken more chances." Why wait until you are 85 to take a chance? Our elders are speaking to us and sharing what they know for sure. I am not saying be reckless but I am saying do not dismiss change. Evaluate the risk—calculate the risk and if it seems and feels good, go for it. What do you really have to lose?

I have been asked, "What did you risk when you started your own business?" I answered, "Nothing. I had very little and I had very little to lose." My grandfather always said, "Build your company (career) in your 20's and 30's when you have little to lose and lots of energy." Now that I am in my 40's what is my risk? The next 20 years? I always have the same answer, "Nothing."

I have no intention of losing. I hate to lose. I do however, like most, love to win.

In the early days, I found myself with a cash flow problem for the first time and feared the worst. When I met with a mentor for advice on this, he laughed. He said all I needed was to spend the money differently and all ended up well. I bring this up because being on the brink of money problems there was fear; however, in resolving the problems, I embraced change.

SET AND ASK FOR EXPECTATIONS AND PROVIDE MEANINGFUL FEEDBACK

"You, me or nobody is gonna hit as hard as life. But it ain't about how hard ya hit, it's about how hard you can get hit and keep moving forward…"

— *Rocky Balboa*

Third grade for me consisted of a mixed bag of low and high expectations stirred with both meaningful and potentially debilitating feedback.

"Jeff is a nice boy, but he will never learn to read." That is what my third grade teacher told my parents. Odd thing about her assessment, rarely was I on her radar. I say this because my best bud Steve and I were so disengaged we would skip her class (yeah in third grade) at every opportunity. My parents, when telling this story, also share how ironic it is that third grade was also the year, "Jeff won the chess championship." I cannot say I was bothered in the least by my teacher's assessment of my future. I know having the unconditional support of my parents kept that nonsense from penetrating my young psyche. Can you imagine the damage it could have done without a strong support system?

Maybe this educator sized me up for errantly because I did not fit her preconceived notion of what high achievers acted or looked like. Maybe she came to this conclusion because she knew nothing about me or maybe because she mistook my short attention span for low IQ. Fortunately, my dad had instilled the first set of Tovar fundamentals into me: 3Ds—Desire, Drive and Determination. Did not matter what this teacher thought, my Dad knew I had the winning combination.

I went on to graduate from college, author and publish study on the beef cattle industry at age 19 (as well as other works) and achieved a MBA. Oh, just for the record, I read 10-20 books a year.

This is why you have to communicate with people. Not everyone has the same expectations as you. You cannot assume that and be successful, in my opinion. Approach life with an open-mind and ask rather than assume what you may think to be true in creating expectations.

Bet you never thought someone like Walt Disney had to deal with low expectations and doubt. The now iconic animator, screenwriter and entrepreneur who created the Disney empire—certainly did. Back in 1927, Disney made several failed attempts to land a distribution deal for his cartoon characters with a huge studio in the industry. MGM Studios told Disney the idea would *never work*—a giant mouse on movie screens would terrify women! (Hollywood Stories—Stephen Schochet)

Amazing—what one assumes as fact can negatively influence situations and people's lives. Today the Disney business brand gives homage to—and masters the principle of exceeding expectations —for its gazillion customers. Exceptional customer service is the heart of the *Disney On Stage and Off Stage* strategy. Disney-esque in spirit, at the heart of TSP, heroic customer service is the heart and soul of our on stage and off stage strategy. We pride ourselves on delivering an exceptional snow removal experience for our customers. While different in scale and industry, both organizations have similar customer-centric cultures embedded in their organizations.

In an organizational culture with happy customers, there are also mostly happy employees. Where the norm for turnover of seasonal workers in the entertainment/theme park industry is 100%, Disney's turnover rate is 22%. Their management turnover is low as well—six percent.

TSP excels with a low employee turnover rate in the snow removal industry as well.

TOVAR WAY FUNDAMENTAL: SET AND ASK FOR EXPECTATIONS

I am a believer in straight-talk given with care and compassion. The fact is (we) people do not know everything and people (we) definitely do not know what is in someone else's mind. In order to reach a consensus of expectations it is very helpful to go over the actual steps of the snow removal process, from truck dispatch to departure, possible concerns, billing, payments, etc...

If you are not clear about what a person wants, ask. Snow can be fun, beautiful and dangerous. Other than TSP snow trucks showing up to remove the snow, ask "What are the top three areas of concern the customer wants TSP to address? What do they expect to gain from this service, this experience, this relationship?" Flat-out, ask. Assume nothing. You are not (nor are you expected to be) a mind reader.

We judge situations not by what happens, but how they compare to what we *expected* to happen. Nearly every misunderstanding can be traced to a difference in expectations. Learn to create mutually understood expectations in every situation.

What were you expecting and why?

I know I'm repeating myself but we are hands-on at TSP. While we were growing by leaps and bounds, so were the expectations of our customers. When we had our initial meeting with a new level of customer, we saw servicing it was going to be different from what we had been accustomed to. Before this client, we landscaped and plowed small strip malls and lots of townhome associations. The work and service expected by our then customers was mostly routine and predictable.

Then upward growth catapulted us into a higher level customer with much higher maintenance expectations. The bar was raised. A new customer wanted us on site for micro lawn observations like dust of dirt blown out of the flowerbed onto the lawn edge, and even for 'dust of snowfall' which is powder light, does not stick and quickly blows away. A client with these kinds of demands was new to us, and at the time, the pressure was over-bearing. Still, we operated with smiles, efficiency and smooth sailing. We delivered what our customer expected with a compassionate attitude and a smile.

Every industry has its own personality. The temperament between businesses in landscaping and snow removal is polar opposite: baseball vs. football. We were challenged in different ways as our business progressed into the snow-only mode. The weather and satellites were now essential instruments. The radar tracks the snow, we are on alert, the call comes in, and with high energy somewhat like fire fighters on duty. We are pumped to respond immediately as we jump into the trucks, drive the distance and do our thing to provide a safer environment. What a rush!

We wanted to learn, we wanted to be the best. We wanted to evolve. We did not close our eyes to this new demanding customer although many, many times it was tempting! We were determined to learn and grow from the experience. We put our aggravations aside and analyzed the situation.

We looked at the numbers.

We compared what it took us to service this customer's over-the-top expectations. The reality? We exceeded his demands without multiple manpower and equipment. This one high maintenance account made our company almost 75% more in revenue than any other one account at the time.

What had we been thinking?

From this elevated level of expectation, a niche was conceived that few snow removal companies had. *Tovar's Zero Tolerance* © ™ (ZT) service was born. Conceptually, ZT was an epic turning point, which landed us into the healthcare facilities snow removal business.

ZT is a system that includes fast dispatch of employees to a site. The customer with the high maintenance expectations turned out to be the inspiration for significant growth.

Expectations that are exceeded result in customer satisfaction and positive reviews. Expectations that are not met result in a disillusioned customer who may not return and reviews that hurt.

However, when setting expectations, start with the expectations we have for ourselves. The goals we set personally and professionally.

TOVAR WAY FUNDAMENTAL: REGULARLY PROVIDE MEANINGFUL ACKNOWLEDGEMENT AND APPRECIATION

How you say something and what you say goes a long way in providing meaningful feedback, acknowledgement and appreciation. Tone and choice of words can make all the difference when it comes to how your feedback is received and perceived.

Catching people doing things right is more effective than catching them doing things wrong. Positive feedback is a tremendous motivator. Regularly give, receive and ask for meaningful (timely, specific, impactful) acknowledgement and appreciation—in all directions throughout the organization. "Good decisions come from experience. Experience comes from bad decisions. It is always too soon to quit," Author unknown.

People sometimes avoid giving meaningful feedback when it may involve conflict and/or confrontation. In a situation involving a TSP manager a few years ago, they found themselves in a position where they did not have the proper documentation to legally dismiss a difficult, non-productive employee. His personnel file did not include any record of excessive lateness or negative behavior. The employee's supervisor had not provided this employee with meaningful feedback or warnings of possible dismissal if things did not change. How could we dismiss him if we had not documented our concerns, expectations and feedback and give him a chance to improve?

My dad, whose parents were born in Mexico, preached his 3Ds to me until those positive fundamentals penetrated my mind and became part of me. My mother, whose parents were from Norway, passed on her love for animals to me. My mother raised golden retrievers, mostly named after Greek gods when I was growing up, and we would walk them together. We rode horses together as well. My parents flooded me with positive meaningful feedback, "Oh Jeff can do this, and Jeff can do that. Good job, Son." This was their style of parenting and it was and is priceless. It is how I raise my daughters. Funny side note: when my dad explained to my oldest daughter the "Three D's"— Drive, desire and determination at the age of six, she responded, "But grandpa, I can't drive yet, I don't have my license!" You better believe that by the time she was eight years old she could drive a pickup truck. Today at the age of fifteen, she drove home from her drivers permit test in crazy traffic as if she had been driving all her life; well, almost all her life.

For me, as a business owner and a parent, giving and getting meaningful acknowledgement and appreciation is an effective leadership tool. I give feedback in the way I would want to be treated. I once had a C-Suite executive tell me so *cavalier* that she motivated her 'troops' by focusing on the two percent they did wrong versus the 98% they did right. She would not be the right fit for TSP.

I am a strong believer that we must focus on our positives. For me, goal setting and positive focus work hand in hand. Strengthen your positive approach by taking in the stories of positive, successful people from all walks of life.

I give my Human Resources department this definition of who is a good fit for our company, "I hire optimists, people with a positive outlook on life. Skills can be taught to a person with a great attitude. It is difficult to teach anything to a person with a negative attitude."

Providing meaningful acknowledgement and appreciation is a major part of the success equation for improvement and growth in an upward and positive direction.

Speak Straight and Listen Generously

'Most people do not listen with the intent to understand;
they listen with the intent to reply.

— *Stephen R. Covey,*
The 7 Habits of Highly Effective People

S peaking straight (or straight talk) should result in galvanizing the team. Confrontation, conflict and consequences are uncomfortable for most people to manage. However, name-calling and meanness is out of order and usually ignites the fire instead of extinguishing it. Speaking out and calling someone profane names without considering the consequences are juvenile knee-jerk reactions. As tempting as it may be to shout out "You 'MF'!" or throw a punch, these gestures lack restrain, finesse and do not promote real resolution. If it has come to the point you say, "Ok, 'MF' let's have a straight talk" you probably have waited way too long to address an issue.

I have found, people usually know what has to be said (and done), yet they will dance all around the obvious. We avoid conflict and confrontation like the plague instead of saying what needs to be said and doing what needs to be done. Sometimes speaking straight may expose vulnerability or admit a need for help.

"You must speak straight so that your words may go as sunlight into our hearts," said Cochise, Tribal Chief, Concahua Apaches.

As experience has confirmed for me, 'to speak from the side of your mouth' or with 'a forked tongue' (a Native American phrase), is a sure way to fuel chaos and confusion in your life and in the workplace.

TOVAR WAY FUNDAMENTAL: SPEAK STRAIGHT

Speak honestly in a way that moves action forward. Make clear and direct requests. Say what you mean, and be willing to raise issues or take positions that may result in direct conflict when it is necessary to reach goals. Be quick to clean up misunderstandings directly with the person or people involved.

Often when you reprimand or even have to terminate someone, if done from "a place of compassion and caring," the process adds value to the experiences of the person spoken to as well as to the speaker. Just as it is usually easier to think negatively than positively, it also may be easier to avoid doing 'the dirty work' and thus allowing the person to stay. This is not being fair to the company, the employers, the team or to the employee that should be fired.

In many cases, the employee is not happy but afraid to leave. Remember what we said about the fear freeze. Some people would rather stay and be unhappy in familiar surroundings than pursue happiness some place new. Often asking someone to leave the company is the best thing for them. Sometimes it takes a non-voluntary act to force one to re-evaluate their circumstances and to seek other opportunities that would be a much better fit: maybe even, landing a job they love.

Now of course, most are not going to sing "Kumbaya" after being disciplined or fired. Some people are just determined to be miserable and were never a good fit in the first place for the team and organization's culture. Life stuff happens. Sometimes you have to 'live together' to really discover one's true colors. Accept that some people will never be happy. You cannot save the world.

Then there is the case when speaking straight may mean being transparent. Chris, our head mechanic is a former Drill Sergeant and a brilliant mechanic who is fluent in German. There may be 9000 guys in all of North America who have the expertise on the kind of equipment TSP has. They have an expertise that can rarely be found in the Midwest. TSP has 700 pieces of equipment.

There was a time when he avoided straight talk if it meant asking for help. For him, that would mean he had failed; and his vulnerability exposed for all to see. Speaking straight needed filtering.

"That was a downfall of mine and it is a misunderstanding," he says now. However, with a type 'A' personality who performs miracles on a day-today basis, he kept his needs to himself. During the unprecedented record-breaking snowstorms, everyone was running out of salt. Chris and his team of four mechanics had to dismantle around 45 trucks and recalibrate them from salt spreaders to liquid spreaders, because of the weather conditions. Does this sound like someone who has failed? Hardly. Far too often, we do not speak straight when it means asking for help or what we need.

The approach used in *speaking straight* merits values, deep thought and confidence. What tone of voice is used and what language is chosen in order to explain or respond to something can make all the difference in the world in the outcome of the conversation.

Honesty and accountability are more than buzzwords. Perhaps, having a straight talk policy would have avoided the total demise of an epic corporate scandal finally uncovered by a previously ignored whistle-blower. Ugly corporate scandals that involved Enron launched the domino effect, which also brought down Arthur Andersen—an iconic Chicago-based accounting firm, World Com and Tyco. In this debacle, were glaring examples of how avoidance in speaking straight to customers, external stakeholders and employees/ internal stakeholders imploded.

Somehow, the CYA (cover your ass) attitude prevailed and thus destroyed formidable companies and turned personal lives upside down *with a green-light to say or do anything* to get and/or keep the business and show a profit! The results? Chaos, confusion, suicides, jail time and thousands and thousands of innocent employees strong-armed out of work—many without their pensions (except Arthur Andersen.) Their employee investment plans had been set up to protect their employees' contributions. Ironically, Andersen was eventually vindicated of all accused wrongdoing. However, it was too little, too ate. By the time of the court's judgment, the 100-year plus company known worldwide for its impeccable reputation was shamefully dismantled and scorned.

Although Andersen went away, I can tell the story of an Andersen employee who did a great job, with integrity and hard work. Although, she was scared to death not knowing what was going to happen. She had worked hard for Andersen and was on the fast track to be a partner. When it was apparent Andersen was done, she was on an even faster track to be a partner because of her reputation. Andersen's competitor, KPMG found her and before you knew it, she became a partner at KPMG.

Samuel A. Colbert, author of *Beyond Bullshit* writes, "Straight talk is a caring, other-sensitive, candor-in demand, loyalty-producing, intimacy-escalating, give and take relationship, leading to enhanced personal and organizational productivity."

When you bring forth positive intentions, a synergy works in tandem in the workplace as well as at home.

TOVAR WAY FUNDAMENTAL: LISTEN GENEROUSLY

> "There are two types of people: those who come in a room and say, 'Well, here I am!' and those who come in and say, 'Ah, there you are.'"
>
> — *Frederick Collins*

There is a story I have been told and have told over a hundred times.

A young woman had the chance to sit between the English Prime Minister and an Ambassador to England at a dinner. As the evening went on, each man captivated her. The ambassador told her of all the amazing places *he* had been and all the great things *he* had done.

The Prime Minister on the other hand asked her about all the places *she* had been to and all *she* had done. The next day when telling a friend about her experience the night before, her friend remarked, "They sound like two incredible people. Who do you think was more intelligent and a better leader?" Without hesitation, the young woman answered, "Who do *you* think? The man who spoke of all his amazing life or the man who listened to me and made me *feel* amazing?" The point is we all want to be heard. Give someone the gift of listening sometimes and you may be amazed as to what may come out of it.

Listening is more than not speaking; it's giving undivided attention to the needs and priorities of others. Set aside your own judgments and preconceived notions. Listen with care and with empathy. There is no one size fits all.

Greek philosopher Epictetus made a profound statement eons ago when he said, "we have one mouth and two ears for a reason." There is a distinct difference between listening and hearing. Listening requires focus not only on the words spoken but also in the unspoken, intended thought. In that regard, face-to-face communication adds a dimension that cannot be substituted by voice-only ones. How else can one observe body language, such as crossed-arms, fidgeting, eyeball shifts?

I am a big listener who still believes strongly in face-to-face contact. My philosophy is anything you want to do has already been done by someone. I seek that person out, listen, and learn.

In connecting with customers, it is very important to remain flexible. In other words, approach each situation without preconceived judgments, barriers and/or experiences. Hard to do? Absolutely but practice makes perfect.

We also listen to our customers and employees through surveys and focus groups. A couple of years ago we found a growing concern from our customers regarding chemicals vs. green. This led to our creation of our own enviro-blend chemical, which is much more environmentally friendly than just plain rock salt. Everyone uses salt, so we adapted our spreaders to use fewer chemicals for the same job. By listening, we continue to evolve and find solutions on how to deliver a product our customers want.

Straight talk and listening have the ability to make all areas of our lives better. Unless you are a hermit, you will interact with others. Those interactions can net out (results after expenses) positive or negative results. It is so easy to blame others and/or feel victimized for our negative results. Excuses of any kind do not change the negative result.

Even today I continue to work on *my* communications skills after multiple academic degrees and twenty-plus years of business experience and exposure! There is always more to learn. I currently work with four business and life coaches. Why? Because, I know I do not know everything there is to know. I am a life-long learner and close listener. These coaches work with me to be a better father, friend, and businessperson and most importantly, just to be a better human being with better results. The focus is always communication and interaction with people. Business is not about bricks and mortar, steel and glass. Business is about people and relationships who work inside the bricks and mortar, steel and glass.

"Jeff reaches out to a stranger (if need be), to people he does not know who have the outcome he wants to have in his business, in his life. He tells them, he wants to talk with them about how they do what they do. The thing about Jeff, when he asks he is respectful and listens to what these people have to say. Humility increases one's odds in gaining a mentor." (Giselle Chapman)

My take-away from learning and listening is that the level of ability that has me to where I am today will not get me to where I need to go tomorrow. My mentor Mike Rorie showed me that by example.

Mike had grown his company from zero to $30 million before he sold it for an undisclosed fortune to Brickman Landscape. After the sale, he worked for them for a bit and then left.

After his non-compete contract expired—typically five years after a sale of a company—and he was somewhat bored with a life of leisure, he re-started his business and after one year did $2 million. I asked Mike how long it had taken him the first time to make $2 million. He laughed and said, "12 years!"

What was different this time? Armed with experience and insight, Mike had listened and was able to grow much faster the second time around. He was still involved with business groups and a continuous thirst for learning and listening. He told me he was doing it very different from the first time because he kept learning. Thus, an already extraordinarily successful man open to growth and change has catapulted Mike to a whole other level.

"The goal of listening well is to achieve win-win communication. Listening well says you care, you are serious about your business, you are open to change and you gain employee and customer loyalty." Terry Wildermann, The Art of Listening.

Be a Rock that Others Can Count On and Be for Each Other

"The more I help others achieve what it is they want, the more others help me achieve what I want."

— *Jeff Tovar*

You can depend on me. Is that not a profound statement of reassurance? A statement evokes a sigh of relief from most people.

Why is dependability important? Because it is important to the people you serve and if you truly serve people, you will be compensated greatly. However, I believe that if you do it just for compensation, the compensation never comes as great as it could. The effort has to be sincere and come from the heart. It cannot be an act. It has to be genuine.

Look, sometimes you have to rev yourself up first to open up your sincerity. Almost like an actor who must focus first to capture the feelings of a character they are about to portray. You may have just gotten off the phone with your teenage son who has rear-ended someone's car in the mall and you need to switch gears on a dime, to dig deep into the heart of a matter with a customer, co-worker and/or a friend.

If you have to use your acting skills at first to get you going, then be an actor until it becomes real. People will respond positively and usually pay a lot to have their problems solved.

When you don't hold back and people know they can count on you, you bring great value to the organization and to yourself.

TOVAR WAY FUNDAMENTAL: BE A ROCK THAT OTHERS CAN COUNT ON

People depend on us to be there when they need us most. Reliability is a must-have not a maybe. What we do or don't when we get that call puts the health and safety of people on the line. It is our job to give them peace of mind. If we make a promise based on what people want to hear versus what can be done, the promise will blow up in our faces. People expect us to be consistent and dependable, like a rock.

When that is compromised, then the question arises, can we be trusted?

People depend on us to be clear, strong, organized and truthful. Actions speak louder than words. Ultimately, you are what you do, not what you say.

This profound statement is on the TSP website under "Blizzard Contingency." It reads, "A blizzard consists of high winds, freezing temperatures and eight (8) or more inches of snow. This does not scare or stress us. We stand ready for snow. In fact, we are so prepared we have backup generators to keep our offices up and running. Trust us to be there."

We are not suggesting that our work saves lives like a surgeon, fire fighter, or Navy Seal. However, when we do our work correctly and on time, we can say we contribute greatly to the safety of many people. Thus, it is essential that we have a powerful camaraderie with each other. Our team, as well as our customers, counts on us.

Chris Polcyn is our head mechanic and his team is literally the rock behind the scene. After 18 years in the military, Chris knows how to get things done under enormously pressurized situations. "This is not a business for 9-5ers or those who live a pre-planned life. Call us a fire department or ambulance service. It is our job to create a safer environment for people. During snow season, I am ready to bunker down, even if I have to sleep on a cot, shower in the office and live off what is in the mini-refrigerator! My attitude is—bring it!"

"Our team is there for each other. We handle trucks being destroyed by the elements, sideswiped and backed into. Instead of strangling those drivers, I know it is a zoo out there, I tell them to go get a burger and I will get it fixed. We cover thousands of miles. People look to us. They depend on our group to make conditions safe. Our work ethic rocks! Bottom line, when equipment is broken, we need to get it fixed. We don't worry about the what, when and why it happened. The reality is, 'it's broke. Get it fixed. At peak times, that can happen twenty to thirty times a day."

I have hundreds of contacts in my phone and with the slide of a button, I can connect with my mentors, coaches, trusted doctors, physical therapists, family, friends, trusted customers, landscapers, contractors, competitors, attorneys, accountants, vendors, etc. These people are 'rocks' that I count on. When I call them, they are right there every time. It is great to have a team to work with whether for a product, information or resources.

Relationships matter more than you may realize. It takes a lifetime to develop these relationships. Once you have them, they are like gold, treat them as such.

Steve, VP of Operations is *the go to guy* for being ready to roll. He lines up everything from equipment maintenance and purchasing with a team of people that depending on the situation, can number 1200 people at several geographical branches. Regional supply depots are set up so snow removal crews do not have to wait long for delivery of supplies such as de-icing chemicals.

Henry, Resource Manager and his mechanics spend spring and summer months assessing the condition of TSP's fleet of trucks and other equipment after a season of plowing: engines, mufflers, brakes, etc.

For the most part, people remain part of the TSP team for a long while. The TSP team is a rock and counts on each other.

Remember Mike Rorie's story? Relationships paid a major role in how he was able to make $2 million in one year instead of twelve years. The knowledge gained and the contacts made along the way are huge. These are the rocks you build your career on. Are you building on a foundation of rocks or mud? It is your choice and the only way to surround yourself with rocks is to be a rock that people can count on.

TOVAR WAY FUNDAMENTAL: BE FOR EACH OTHER

I believe being a rock ties into being there for each other. If you are a rock, you can support others when they need someone to lean on. There is a lack of mentality in the world today that is like a virus; what it is spreading is that for me to have more, means someone else has to have less. The reality is there is plenty of good stuff to go around for everyone. Do you perceive your glass to be half-empty or half full?

Support each other's success. Work from the point of view that we're all in this together and none of us can win at the expense of someone else on the team. Look for the best in each other, and provide rigorous support when it's needed, including honest and direct feedback.

Rick Lenth talked about his light bulb moment during a collaborative training session. "*I'd been working with some people internally and had become frustrated. I would give them what they asked for but I wouldn't go the extra mile to help them succeed. I just did my job and gave nothing more. The coach was telling us to help them when you see them going off the trail, not just what they asked for, but help them succeed. And I realized I wasn't being as helpful as I could be.*

I had kind of shut down on some people; I was just doing the very minimal. I was not comfortable with what I was doing when I knew I could do more to help them succeed. I had just shut down. I stopped caring. I hadn't addressed how well or poorly we were working together. During this coaching session, I decided to address the way I was handling things. I went back and started helping people succeed.

When I opened up with them, I decided to let go of any frustrations. If I couldn't let it go then I had some uncomfortable conversations that I had been avoiding. That decision took the burden off what had been holding me down. People then became aware of how certain behavior affected me since we talked it out, we started working better together.

The change in me had begun with a coach in a collaborative training session. It forced me to change.

When I accepted my part in how the team was working, and realized I would get frustrated and shut down, then I could see I was holding myself back by holding on to some negative energy. When I decided to open up, it was like a valve opened and everyone worked much better together. I had to admit that how I handled things made an impact: good and bad..."

I have found that many of the most successful people are more than happy to tell you how they became successful. It usually is not a secret. Many believe by sharing information and helping others, they will help themselves. This fact is evident by all the books written by successful people. They understand the value in helping others. The act of sharing adds to their riches and enrichment.

Our team has its share of snow stories. From a logistics point of view, we operate a lot like the fire department in how we handle things: big and small. We have been in minus 10 temperatures when salt spreaders freeze up and had to resort to a shovel and pick axe to get the job done. In the beginning, there was one shift called 'however long it took to get the job done.' An ice storm came in 1997 while I was at a weeklong conference in Hawaii. Did I ever live that one down? Anyway, Steve remembers it well, "The ice storm kept going on and off for three to four days. We were not set up for a storm such as this. But we made the commitment and we had to work the storm until it was over. We had to be there for each other."

We needed to make things better for our team. It was a brutal lesson but in typical TSP style, a lesson learned led to a stronger organization. We knew we had to change our model. We changed our operations. We learned we needed to have enough people ready to handle whatever the type of load. That experience gave us more wisdom and insight in an area that needed our attention and action. We know now that no matter what the situation we must be better prepared and the overall well-being of the TSP team comes first.

Realize all good things come in time. Sam Walton said, "I was a 40 year overnight success." For me, it is about being successful every day. Success, like life, is not a destination but a journey. If you will only be happy if success comes quickly than your happiness will also go away quickly.

I say, enjoy the ride—it is fascinating. Part of enjoying the ride is enjoying the people you surround yourself with. Remember this quote, "When the wrong people leave your life, the right things start happening."

When you truly care about others, others will care about you. In return, those around you help you achieve what you want because you have helped them. This is a rule of the Universe. By helping others, you help yourself and your life becomes magical.

FACE CHALLENGES HEAD ON AND LOOK FOR THE POSITIVE

"Being challenged in life is inevitable, being defeated is optional."

— *Roger Crawford*

There is research that suggests that 85% of the population vibrates to a negative frequency and that is how the human brain is wired. Thus, the TV news model, 'if it bleeds it leads' regarding the selection process of the lead story to pull in the audience. On the flip side, there is growing research that the vibrations of positive energy and expectations that successful people give off (emit) actually attract to them the very experience they believe they are going to get. (want)

I remember telling a reporter for Snow Magazine, "...one of the key things we're always talking about is to be relentless about continuous improvement. (That is what giving and asking for feedback is all about.) Constantly evaluate and re-evaluate everything you do and don't be satisfied with the status quo. The most successful organizations are in a constant cycle of improvement. I'm constantly trying to get better."

I do not believe in worrying needlessly about the what-ifs in life. We often spend too much time and energy on worrying about things that are not as bad as we thought or circumstances out of our control. Our energy is our source of power, like our own personal electricity, and once we realize that, we value it and do not want to waste it. The fact of the matter is, too many of us live in the world of what-if rather than being present in the world of what-is. Living in what-if avoids facing challenges. Living in what-if is a cop-out.

Facing challenges for me means stop being afraid. People tell me I am different, or they are not at my level financially, so they cannot act like I act. I have had my ups and downs financially, but I know it will always end up all right. My kids will eat. I once told this guy that if I had to start over and delivering pizzas was the only job I could get, I would deliver pizzas to feed my kids. The guy chimed in that even though I would be a delivery guy, I would be thinking about the big picture and how to be the owner of the pizza place and eventually the pizza chain. I had to laugh, because he was point on, I look for the positive outcome.

I do not feel I am different from other hard-working middle class people. By no means have I lived a charmed life. My 3rd grade teacher had all but written me off as a kid who would never learn how to read.

Can you take a punch like that? I think at some point, I decided to stop being afraid. Then one day, my Dad's friend, Mr. Bullaro, gave me great advice—take the first punch. *"A man (woman) never knows what he (she) is made of until you get punched. When you take the first punch, you learn quickly how to survive: to keep your chin down, you keep moving and you never stop swinging,"* writes author Billy Coffey. Believe me, things turned out much better after that advice, maybe too good. The good news is that I outgrew the stupid kids' stuff.

TOVAR WAY FUNDAMENTAL — FACE CHALLENGES HEAD ON

Do not blow challenges off or assume the worst. Face challenges head on and find solutions. Stuff happens. Life is messy. Setbacks are nothing more than speed bumps on the road to success. See problems as opportunities to be heroic. It's not what happens, but how we respond that defines us. Make the impossible possible. Work at it. Stay positive.

TSP's Chuck Haas talks about how TSP faced challenges head on and found solutions in a historic winter. *"This fundamentally sums up every winter storm that we work. The storms never hit exactly like the weathermen predict and therefore we are continually adapting and adjusting. Aside from the day-to-day challenges, one large obstacle in the winter of 2013/14 was the salt shortage. This was a topic that spanned across the Midwest and newspapers and evening anchormen alike talked about the severity of the situation. Some municipalities and many of our competitors completely ran out of chemical. That wasn't an option that Tovar was willing to entertain. Sure, the chemical was hard to get, we* had to travel further to get it, and it cost us more, but we made a commitment to our customers to keep their lots safe and we honored that commitment. Furthermore, we utilized more liquid applications in our process. Due to the fact that we are able to manufacture our own liquids and that the manufacturing process requires less bulk product than a typical chemical application, this was yet another solution to the salt shortage allowing us to stretch the product's usefulness. We then retro-fit all of our trucks to have liquid capabilities and it was back to business as usual."

Dr. Grandin of Colorado State University has faced unbelievable diversity in her life. When Temple Grandin was a young girl in 1950, she was labeled autistic, which was a sure road, especially in the 1950s, to a life spent in a mental institution. However, her strong-willed, optimistic mother would challenge the status quo and fought for Temple's right to lead a quality and positive life. Not only has she overcome autism, but had greater victory becoming a female leader in agriculture; an industry considered a male-dominated world. Today, Dr. Temple Grandin is a Professor of Animal Science at Colorado State University and an international expert on livestock handling facility design.

I had the opportunity to work with Dr. Grandin as a student at Colorado State when I wrote and published a paper on the beef cattle industry. She has a brilliant mind and I learned all I could from her. There were no signs of autism holding her back. "I am different, not less," says Dr. Grandin.

I believe **the key** component to success more than anything else is one's attitude. Money can be a component of success. Relationships can be a component; education can be a component, as can other things. However, your attitude plays into all of the above. Consider this. If you think your life sucks then it probably does. If you think your life is good—it most likely is.

Our business relationships, like personal ones sometimes take time to develop. Our relationship with JP Morgan started with plowing one branch. It was only one branch, but we believed that if we took excellent care for them, they would give us more business. We currently service over 300 branches as customers.

Challenges are often opportunities leading to better things.

TOVAR WAY FUNDAMENTAL—LOOK FOR THE POSITIVE

You have the power to choose your attitude. You will get whatever you focus your attention on. Look for the good in things. Be optimistic and see the possibilities. Optimism creates positive energy and positive energy creates success.

Do you get what you look for? A friend challenged me to take one day and only look for the positive in another friend. Then the next day to only look for the negative. Long story short, the first day was an incredible day spent with the most amazing person on the planet. Day two, I was ready to kill them! I went back to the positive outlook and day two got better. Just goes to show you, 'you get what you look for.'

The expectation of a positive outcome when dealing with a challenging situation or person is NOT the same as living in a fantasy world, or having pipe dreams. The expectation is as real as the air we breathe.

There is scientific proof that positive thoughts and intentions can alter the physical world around us. Through our thoughts, words and action, we are able to create the choice of having a positive perspective versus a dark, heavy, and draining one. Our attitudes are guided by the choices we make; such as the people in our inner circle, what we think about, as well as those things we say and how we say them. Those same attitudes are influenced by what we watch online, on TV, at the movies and your choice of music.

What does your energy say about you? Does it represent the true you?

The shapes and movement of water samples document the power of energy on thoughts, words and deeds. Research by Dr. Masuru Emoto from Japan demonstrated how 2000 people focused on positive or negative thoughts while focused on distilled water formations could change the water's molecular composition. This was documented by a series of astonishing photographs.

Water makes up 60% of the human body and 70% of our brains. During Dr. Emoto's study, when positive thoughts and emotions such as love and compassion were focused on the water displayed delicate, symmetric structures. When the water was sent negative emotions (like fear and unrest), the molecular structure of the water changed to chaotic, fragmented ripples. The evidence provided by studies in the science of neuroplasticity, shows our thoughts can change the structure and function of our brains.

An uncle of mine would always say, "If I didn't have bad luck, I wouldn't have any luck at all." He seemed to look for reasons to say it because he felt his luck was bad and good things just did not come his way. He was always sick with something. Even when something positive would happen to my uncle it was never enough and never celebrated by him.

My mentor, Dr. Bernard Rollin encouraged us to celebrate even the little things in life.

A friend would often say, "So what if I am out of shape, one day I will get some sort of cancer, have a little chemo and I will lose the weight and life will be better." Well, I bet you can guess what he got for this 40th birthday.

Why would anyone what to conjure up cancer and bad luck?

Expect good things. I do and I would not tell you to do something I do not do. I expect to make lots of money. I expect to have the love of my children. I expect to have many great friends and to be a great friend and father. I expect this book to help my employees, my children, and others who might gravitate to it and me.

All those good things will happen. I truly live a blessed life and have so many other good things coming my way. No way am I saying my life is perfect, but I focus on the good and get good back into my life multiplied.

I had a potentially unpleasant issue come up at work. I expected a positive result and had not lost any sleep over it. The negotiations to this issue adopted the attitude of win/win from the onset. The outcome came from a place of love and friendship. It could have been very ugly.

You have the power to choose your attitude. You will get whatever you focus your attention on. Look for the good things, be optimistic and see the possibilities. Optimism creates positive energy and positive energy creates success.

Positive attracts positive. Negative attracts negative. In the book, *The Secret* for example, there is a lot of talk about the law of attraction: what you think about, you attract. Some people dismiss this theory as ridiculous hocus-pocus, yet many would not hesitate to accept theories of quantum physics based on the same principal.

Whether the challenges are presented by acts of God or acts of man, many back away from challenges, believing conflict will be at the heart of the matter. They would rather wish it away by doing nothing or by pretending it does not exist. Few of us, look forward to dealing with challenges head-on. Few of us like to 'put ourselves out front' in challenging situations but the sentence made famous by iconic boxing legend Joe Louis says it all, "you can run but you can't hide."

Norman Doidge, MD has evidence to prove that repetitive positive thoughts and activity can rewire and strengthen the brain. In his book, *The Brain That Changes Itself: Stories of Personal Triumph from the Frontier of Brain Science,* cites evidence that supports positive thinking results as scientific fact.

So then, when given the choice, why not always look for the positive in work, people, situations and life in general.

I remember in the movie, *When Harry Met Sally*, Sally says to Harry, "You are Mr. Doom & Gloom." To which Harry replies, "All I am saying is that when the shit comes down I am going to be ready." Although taken from romantic comedy at that, I do agree that one should be prepared to face challenges. Harry goes on to say, "I have spent days, weeks, months, focusing on the dark side." Who wants to worry about bad crap *that* much? Just do not dwell on the bad things, instead dwell on the good things. If nothing else, you will be happy up to the time the bad thing occurs.

Zig Ziglar says it well, "Your attitude, not your aptitude, will determine your altitude."

Always Think Big and Be Passionate About Quality

"The great danger for most of us is not that we aim too high and fall short but rather we aim too low and achieve it."

— Michelangelo

When I was asked by a friend recently, "So, is it your goal to be a billionaire?" I answered immediately, "NO!" That is not a goal, it will just happen because of other goals. Some may think it cocky to say we will be a billion dollar company but I don't think it is. By saying it and believing it, it will happen. In this life, you get what you expect to get. Most people do not get much; because they don't expect much.

People always outweigh or overthink the risk. They want a great plan, a roadmap. something that tells them exactly what to do, step by step. They want a guarantee that they will succeed. Having a guarantee never concerned me or prevented me from moving forward. I would cream big and go to work to achieve it.

"In a moment of decision the best thing to do is the right thing, the next best is the wrong thing, and the worst thing you can do is to do nothing." — Teddy Roosevelt

TOVAR WAY FUNDAMENTAL: ALWAYS THINK BIG

Aim high. Set and write down goals. Challenge yourself to achieve more than you ever thought possible. Only big goals have the power to inspire us. Expect to succeed in a big way, and then make it happen. I have written down my goals for years. Once I write them down, most of them happen.

You cannot get to second base with both feet on first. Dream big and go to work. Activate the dream. I have found that you need to get to work and adjust as you go. A friend said to me that he would have started a company if only he had known what to do. Well the truth of the matter is no one really knows what to do until you start the process. You MUST start. This is not to suggest one should start anything without a plan or thought, to the contrary. I am just saying do not sabotage the start because you are locked into a perpetual planning mode. *"I've been with TSP for 21 years," said Rick Lenth, VP Administration, "during a strategic planning meeting about 10 years ago, we had just read a book called* Good to Great, *in which the idea of BHAGS (Big, Hairy, Audacious Goals) was discussed. So during our planning session the conversation changed from setting a comfortable goal which we were pretty certain we could meet, to instead, setting a goal which seemed very far reaching. Like the story of the kids who were trying to throw rocks over the roof of the house and missing every time. Then one kid came who was trying to throw rocks over the moon, and missed, but was able to throw it over the house while he was trying for the moon. The moral of the story being 'shoot for the moon, you might not reach the moon but you will land among the stars.'*

What's fun is every 5 years the company ends up looking completely different. Since change is constant for us, you know it's going to change, but you don't know how it's going to change. In everything we do; we are going to get better at it the next time around. We feed off of each other, as changes happen they spur other areas to change. We each bring different aspects to the table that seem to complement each other.

Frankly, I thought 'a comfortable goal' was a bit boring after the idea of BHAGS was mixed into the conversation. So we decided to set our goal to grow TSP to $100M. To get to that goal, we just can't do the status quo. We had to get into a different way of thinking in order to go after it. No one was really comfortable with the goal, but we got comfortable chasing that idea. It wasn't an immediate buy in, but we liked the concept of being challenged. We like to think we are open to change, even though thinking big means rapid growth. Rapid growth brings risk and headaches. But then, it's who we are: 100% growth vs. 10% growth? Easy answer, go after 100%."

As you build your network of people around you, maybe someone knows a person who has achieved what you want. It is all right to ask them if they will make an introduction. Recently, I asked several people in my various networks to help me meet Sir Richard Branson. A couple of friends took the challenge and it is a goal I will achieve. Talk about a guy who seems to be having fun in business!

You will be amazed how people will share their steps to success with you. Be a willing student. There is a Zen saying, "When the student is ready, the teacher will appear."

Approach a potential mentor from your heart space with humility and respect. Almost anything, you may want to achieve, you can find someone who has already achieved it. Ask them how they did it. In addition, think about what value you may bring to a mentor. A good attitude means everything, and increases one's odds with much sought after mentors.

I had lots and lots of help. By no means can I sit here and tell you I did this and built this and did everything by myself. I'm the luckiest person in the world. I've had tons and tons of help from lots of smart people. Luck is said to be the result of preparation and opportunity meeting. I challenged myself through life and sports since I was a kid. I was always in motion, a trait I believe I got from my mother. My grandfather would always say, "Build your career in your 20's when you have the energy to work hard, and when you are older you will have built something that can make money by working more with your head and less with your back." I put that advice into practice.

Practice makes perfect. In Malcolm Gladwell's book, *Outliers*, he identifies the 10,000 rule for success, which states it takes 10,000 hours of practice to become an expert in any competition whether in music composition, creating Facebook to winning a gold medal. The rule has to do with attaining big time success based on Anders Ecrisson's analysis of people like John Rockefeller, Tiger Woods, and Bill Gates (to name a few).

In The New Yorker Gladwell posted, "it's not difficult for a young person free from constraints of conventional schooling to spend 10,000 hours in an area of passionate interest."

When you break it down, I spent way more than 10,000 hours mowing lawns and thinking big starting at age 12.

When you're mowing lawns you've got a lot of time to think. I worked business plans in my mind while I was cutting lawns. I probably put together 10 million different business plans in my mind while I was mowing lawns. I remember dreaming someday of having 10 trucks.

When I started high school, I had some friends working for me. I charged $12-15 per lawn and paid my friends $5-6 per hour, a little better than minimum wage 30 years ago. I set goals such as 'cut so many lawns by lunch, so many by 4pm so my 'crew' would wrap up at a decent hour and enjoy the rest of the day. However, I handled maintenance, repairs, bills, etc. after everyone else went home.

Maybe unconsciously, I thought my family needed money since my Dad suddenly had his neck broken, became a quadriplegic and could not work in the beginning. Maybe I just figured out on my own (because no one told me this), that if I wanted to go to school I was going to need money. What I knew and was very conscious of was the math of mowing lawns: people pay $15 to have their lawns mowed and if I mow 10 lawns, I make $150 and if I do 20, I make $300. So I made up flyers and the rest is history.

TOVAR WAY FUNDAMENTAL: BE PASSIONATE ABOUT QUALITY

Henry Ford once said, "Quality means doing it right when no one is watching." We should take pride in the quality of everything we touch and everything we do. We should demand and consistently shoot for quality in our service, our equipment, our training, and our facilities.

TSP's Joe Constantino talks about quality:

"During my first year as an inside sales representative my account manager, Mike Yager, asked if I can prioritize quality over quantity when scheduling appointments. One of our targeted opportunities for this was with a large hospital network in Peoria. Originally, we were only able to get their Request for Proposal for their snow removal bid. I knew that getting the RFP would help me to achieve my goals as an inside sales representative, but I also understood that an RFP by itself does not provide us the best opportunity to solidify a contract.

I wanted to schedule a face-to-face visit. That was my challenge.

My first few calls to them led me to dead ends. Everyone I spoke with was very determined to answer questions either by phone or e-mail. I continued to reach out to different people and different departments to inquire on a possible visit prior to bidding. After a few days of calling with no luck, I was fortunate to get someone on the phone that was willing to listen to reasons why we would like to visit. I took advantage of this opportunity and expressed how valuable a visit would be to putting together our best bid to ensure quality of service. I remember how excited I was to schedule the appointment, but even more so I remember how excited Mike Yager was when I let him know that we had this visit scheduled!

In the end, Mike was able to secure the contract and, importantly, be in the position to deliver quality service. Mike maintains a strong professional relationship with the facilities management team which he developed through constant communication over the years. We have not looked back since."

The Tovar footprint was on all the lawns I mowed as a kid. Mowing lawns gave me something to do. Maybe I was somewhat entrepreneurial (without consciously thinking about it). No matter what, I know I would have ended up doing something.

I learned to walk around the yard at the end of each job and check to see that everything looked up to the standard I had set. I could not leave a job that I did not feel looked great. If you do a great job for people like showing up on time, finishing on time, cleaning up when done, you will not have any major problems. Because I acted as though I was a big company—(remember my Dad with the 3D's: Desire, drive, determination). My dad would joke that I was not a million dollar landscape company with a fleet of 25 trucks. In my mind's eye, I 'saw' myself having a fleet of at least 50 trucks—one day!

Aristotle said, "Quality is not an act; it is a habit." How does a company insure quality when there are so many moving parts? We believe in our products and services and we are very passionate about what we do. We live for snow, and to take care of our customers. Combine that with the innovative change oriented corporate culture and we continually adapt to new market situations and adopt emerging technologies.

TSP executive, Eric Hartmann puts the passion for quality in perspective, *"I think the culture that Jeff has created here is conducive to bringing the best out of people and if you do that, you're going to have the best product. Some of our best ideas have come from salt truck drivers and shovelers. We encourage innovative solutions. It's exciting to see this company grow and exciting to see all the opportunity it has created for all the people. The people make the difference."*

BE A TEAM PLAYER AND CHECK THE EGO AT THE DOOR

*"Great things in business are never done by one person.
They're done by a team of people."*

— Steve Jobs

I like this acronym—T.E.A.M. (**T**ogether **E**veryone **A**chieves **M**ore). I was a competitive swimmer from first to fifth grades and then into high school. Swimming is a great sport but primarily it is an individual one. I was the breaststroke guy and there is no greater way to take complete responsibility than doing an individual sport. However, as I grew older, I found that team sports like baseball and football were more fun. I felt so much joy in playing a team sport. With a team, I was part of something bigger. Individually I could win or lose. As a team member, I could contribute to the whole, cheer on and help my team win.

When you consider great basketball players, Michael Jordan and Larry Bird come to mind. They were leaders on and off the court, in games and in practice. Michael Jordan is known for being the first to arrive and the last to leave, what a great example. Larry Bird is known for being the greatest cheerleader off the court and a great leader on the court.

After college, I switched my game from football to the great game of business. Playing the game of business and doing it well is what gives me "the rush"—adrenaline-pumping-excitement-energy. When I think of playing to win in the snow plowing business game, I do not just think of myself, I think of our team. There is no "I" in TEAM.

When you operate fluidly with a team, your individual ego does not matter in the big picture. What matters is how you use that energy: to unite and collaborate or divide and complicate. I am not saying you become a wuss, but you become a valuable member of a collective. When Quincy Jones and Michael Jackson produced the video, "*We Are the World*" to raise money for African famine relief in 1985, with A-list singers/musicians such as Lionel Richie, Tina Turner, Madonna and many others, Jones tacked a sign on the studio door which read, "Check Your Egos at the Door." The recording sessions went smoothly despite entourages, time limitations, schedule challenges and late-minute artists' contributions.

TOVAR WAY FUNDAMENTAL: BE A TEAM PLAYER

Our success is dependent on our ability to communicate and work together seamlessly. There is no such thing as one person or one department succeeding and another falling short. We win and lose as a team.

Steve and I have worked as a team since the early lawn mowing business. Steve's forte is sales and relationships. Mine is operations. Over time, we developed our skills and excelled at different things. My number one job is to help our team win and take care of our customers. Steve was in charge of sales. Eric Hartmann was in charge of operations and they were both at the top of their game. One day they joked that the other had the hardest job in the company. I was serious when I said, "Steve, you are in charge of operations now and Eric, you are now in charge of sales." Their jaws dropped to the floor but they jumped in and excelled at their new jobs. Now I am certain that Eric is a better salesman than Steve is and vice versa.

As a team, we communicate our goals and action plans to the rest of our team, and strive to accomplish seamless implementation more often than not. When Steve had the fight of his life to win, a fierce cancer diagnosis, our team was on the same page. Because we were, seamless implementation allowed us to keep moving without skipping a beat. Steve's absence left a huge void, not just physically but emotionally as well.

Then life stuff happened again. Now it was I out of commission. I had a brief battle with situational depression—something foreign to me at the time. Like many of us, I had preconceived opinions about depression's causes and effects. When I damn-near killed myself in a snowmobile accident and ripped the muscles and nerves in my leg,

I got an uninvited visit from depression.

Although I survived many crashes and a head-on collision, after three surgeries and chronic pain, I began to drift into a dark, gloomy place. Before this experience, I incorrectly thought depression was an individual, maybe unconscious, choice. Yes, I thought to be depressed were a choice people made. Now through my experience, I learned that is not the case. I became more compassionate: we are all human and have tough times and for me not to judge things I do not understand. Then I realized this dark, unlike Jeff mood began with the pain medication I'd been taking. I stopped cold turkey. My inner sunshine and positive outlook soon reappeared. I acquired a greater understanding of how fragile our chemical balance is and how vulnerable the balance is to outside factors such as medications and stress.

The point is, while I was injured, the TSP team was still in the game and I was able to watch from the sidelines while TSP continued to operate in the black.

With individual sports, if you are hurt, you cannot compete. With team sports, you can win as a player coach, even as an injured player on the sidelines. Win or lose, you do it as a team.

I saw this up close and personal one night. I was at Game 5 of the Chicago Blackhawks battle to get into the Stanley Cup Finals. At the end of three periods, the score was 4-4; at the end of five periods, the Hawks won 5-4 after playing some of the most intense hockey I have ever seen. Not only did the Hawks win, everyone in the United Center won.

The United Center went nuts and it was only after 15 minutes of non-stop cheering that the crowd began to dissipate. In business and life, there are many team victories and many winners. The difference is unlike hockey where only one team can win the Stanley Cup, in life many teams can win.

TOVAR WAY FUNDAMENTAL: CHECK THE EGO AT THE DOOR

Our own egos and personal agendas must never get in the way of doing what is best for the team. Worrying about who gets credit, who looks good, or who looks bad is counterproductive. Make sure every decision is based solely on what will advance our team goals. Do not take challenges personally or defensively. Rather, embrace them as opportunities to increase your contribution to our collective success.

As a defensive end (DE) at Colorado State University, my job was to put pressure on the quarterback or get into the backfield and tackle the ball carrier. The team works in tandem to achieve the goal of winning. I guess you can say I have carried that playbook through to my team.

It is important that the team decision come not from the ego of someone who dominates the group/team process, but comes from the core of the team consensus and/or compromise. A team with an undesirable compromise, led by ego, as in the *groupthink syndrome* happens when a group or team's desire for consensus and cohesiveness, overwhelms its goal of reaching the best possible decision. *One of the most clearly documented examples of groupthink involved the space shuttle Challenger disaster. As NASA was preparing to launch the shuttle, numerous problems and questions arose. (In the adrenaline rush) at each step of the way, decision makers argued that there was no reason to delay and that everything would be fine. Shortly after its launch, the shuttle exploded, killing all seven crewmembers. * (Ricky Griffin, Fundamentals of Management).*

Scary consequences. As you see, problems occur when people are more concerned with personal gain than a team victory, or when a team member is a slacker and not doing their part.

Playing as part of the team is important in sports and business. When individuals play only for themselves, the team is hurt and usually self-destructs.

How many times have you encountered individuals in leadership positions with an "it's for me to know and you to find out" mentality? Jim Paluch, CEO of JP Horizons and author of many books comments on this approach. *"Jeff was always willing to try things. Role-playing, games, brainstorming, pushing himself and his team out of their comfort zone. It is on the edge of our envelope where the greatest learning takes place and the best mentors care enough about the person their working with to challenge them in order to get them into a place where the experience will teach them what they need to know."*

There are many good teams but few great teams.

Great teams have:
1. Common vision
2. Good players that play great
3. Great players that are part of a team first

Take the United States Olympic Hockey Team versus USSR in *The Miracle on Ice*, fierce fight as the underdog to win the gold medal in the 1980 Winter Olympics.

Or take Vince Lombardi's Green Bay Packers versus Dallas Cowboys in 13 degrees in the 1967 Ice Bowl: coming together despite sub-freezing temperatures facing frostbite, ice hazards and injuries to claim a staggering victory, 21-17, for the NFL Championship. No ego there; just the will to play great football and accomplish victory.

It is important that the decisions be based on what is best for the team and not what is best for the team leader's ego. I tell my top team of managers, "We will make decisions as a team. If we cannot agree, I will be the deciding vote and when we leave the conference room, we walk out as a team." If we try to execute and find that maybe I made the wrong decision, I do not let my pride get in the way of making a change. It is always about the team win.

Deliver Heroic Customer Service and Practice Blameless Problem Solving

"If you treat people right, they will treat you right 99% of the time."

— *Franklin Delano Roosevelt*

Years ago, a company that I consider myself a mentee of was featured in a magazine article. The CEO of the company said they were really not innovative. He said they were just really sharp at recognizing a good idea and then copying it. Imitation is the greatest form of flattery. So much of this book is about the impact of mentors in attaining success and taking shortcuts or copying. I have to be honest, 'heroic customer service' was a slogan (term) I learned from reading about a Fortune 500 company. They described 'heroic customer service' and I thought it mirrored our TSP vision.

The snowplow business is a great place for customer service. The basic idea here is to take a potentially terrible weather/business day (as we experienced for many days during the Polar vortex of 2014) and make it a non-issue for our customers. We describe our employees as "Tovar Heroes" and often call Human Resources, "Hero Support."

TOVAR WAY FUNDAMENTAL: DELIVER HEROIC CUSTOMER SERVICE

Simply put, we exist for no other reason than to serve our customers —external and internal. Customers are our lifeblood. We have no jobs without them. Customer satisfaction is for lesser companies. Take the extra steps necessary to blow your customers away with heroic service.

How is our relationship on a scale of one to 10? What would make it a 10? That is the question I want answered when developing relationships and rendering heroic customer service.

For John Chiarella, Jr., owner of Ultimate Grounds in Connecticut says "The Rake" customer service is a top priority. *"We service the customer. Period. Whether it's a weekend night and a frightened client who cannot sleep because of a nest of bumblebees on her sun porch calls and asks could I please send someone there to get rid of them. I went and took care of the problem. I've located a highly desired African Redtail for a customer. I've even helped wrap a few Christmas gifts for clients who found themselves in last-minute time crunches. At my company, we live customer service on a daily basis."*

Having customer service as a priority in an organization speaks volumes about its leadership and culture. Like Starbucks and Southwest Airlines, it is all in how customers are treated. "We aren't in the airline business; we are in the 'Customer Service business' and we just happen to fly airplanes," said Colleen Barrett, former President and COO, of Southwest airlines.

When you look at your job as an extension of yourself, it becomes personal and one becomes more vested in the process.

We have hundreds of examples of heroic customer service, from plowing the roads so ComEd could bus their employees from a hotel to a service center, to rescuing a customer's daughter from a ditch where her car was stuck.

Why such emphasis on delivering heroic customer service? First, it just feels good and second, it changes people's lives for the better. To accomplish this, one must adopt a servant's attitude. Like most things, when you serve, it comes back to you 100 times over. When you give, you get. When you help others, they help you back. Of course, sometimes it may take years of heroic customer service before it comes back, but it always comes back in some fashion.

Why would you do anything less than great service? Usually, the difference between good and great is a little effort. Why shortchange yourself and the customers? Give a great effort and it will eventually come back to you. Most people put forth a good effort for a few days or months and then decide the effort isn't worth what they want to achieve. The paycheck is not there and they get discouraged. They are just about to turn the corner and they walk away or they lower the service. You know what? Just as they are approaching greatness, they give up and settle for mediocre: settling for less than their best. Don't do it!

Tony Robbins said, "When you start out in your career, *the great ones* give 1000 units of effort for 1 unit of reward." (In other words, give much more than you get) Eventually, for every unit of effort given one unit of reward is obtained. Then the pendulum swings the other way and for every one unit of effort, when *the great ones* give, they get 1000 or infinite units of reward. This is an example of how you can become one of the great ones.

Start with yourself. It all begins and ends with you. Take care of yourself and it pays huge dividends. Take care of yourself with proper rest, managed stress, nutrition, exercise and positive mental and emotional stimulation. You must first take care of yourself before you are able to take care of others.

What instructions do flight attendants give to passengers before take-off? They say that in case of loss of oxygen in the cabin, take the oxygen mask and put it on yourself first, and then you are in the position to help others.

The interesting thing is that there is a flywheel effect. Paul Smith of the PS Group explains, "A Flywheel is (a device) used to store energy and once properly in motion, can provide enough energy to power a system with near unstoppable momentum. Companies that consistently pull ahead of the competition have a strong flywheel helping to drive their programs."

The flywheel, in this context, is when you start giving TLC (tender loving care) to yourself, your customers and others the payback may be slower than you would like. I can tell you after years of doing it; the payback (the flywheel) becomes larger than the payout (the effect).

I find most people don't get it. They want to put a dollar in and get a dollar out. If I am worth $10 per hour, I want to be paid $10 for every hour. Instead, give $100 of effort when you are starting out for

$1 of pay. When you do this, eventually the pendulum swings the other way and you get $100 for every $1 worth of effort. Your efforts compound and you do more with less.

TOVAR WAY FUNDAMENTAL: PRACTICE BLAMELESS PROBLEM SOLVING

Blame has no place in a high performance organization. Fix mistakes by focusing on solutions, not on fault. Learn what to do and what not to do from the mistakes made. Then apply that knowledge by improving our processes to reduce the likelihood of repeating the same mistake. Get smarter with every mistake.

Like they say when you are skiing, "if you don't fall sometimes you are not trying hard enough." To make mistakes means you are at least out there learning and the mistake probably will not mean the end of the world. Making mistakes is one thing but not fixing them is another. A time-sensitive fix, not a quick fix, is required.

Taking charge but allowing flexibility and treating people with a sense of humanity makes the greatest difference when dealing with problems, conflict and other challenges.

Making a mistake is hardly an indictment: no shame, no blame. Fixing it is the way we learn.

TSP's Eric Hartmann tells the story about a situation in the early days when TSP first became a snow only business. *"We had a huge client who had been with us since the landscape days. The problem arose when we underpriced their snow plowing needs. Because we were still inexperienced in some aspects of pricing, we ended up in a serious situation. We had different managers then who had done the initial snow plowing estimates. Bottom line...we had to fix it. No excuses, we just were not sophisticated enough in that side of the business at that point and made some important mistakes. We had to go back to our huge client, admit our mistake and tell them we had to increase the price we had contracted for after honoring our commitment for a year. When the contract was up for renewal, we needed to renegotiate the numbers.*

How had we made such a mistake? One thing, we had not measured the clients' properties in a while. Therefore, our guys re-measured all 45 properties. That was the deciding factor. We had under-estimated the size of the properties and thus the amount of time, personnel, equipment and chemicals needed. What we came up with was we had to increase the contracted price by 40%—a big hit for a client. That is how far off our initial estimate was. Therefore, we negotiated to increase their costs 10% over a 4-year period. The client agreed and we thought we were home free.

They fired us. They left us for four months and went to a competitor. Not good. They did come back, with the 40% increase factored into the new cost. We no longer had to stretch out our initial pricing mistake over a four-year period! By doing a great job in the first year, even though TSP lost money, the customer realized no one else could do such a great job for the price we were offering.

Why did they say they came back? They said it was because of TSP's high-level customer service, our heroic customer service!"

Our team action, positive attitude, dedication and blameless problem solving made a significant difference in their decision to come back to TSP.

I have found that some of the best customer relationships come from when our company makes a mistake. What is our procedure when we mess-up with our customer?

1. Say we are sorry, accept blame and do not point fingers.
2. Gain customer agreement on what would fix the problem, and then fix it.
3. Ask the customer for an acceptable time-line to fix the problem.
4. Make certain that customer is happy with the solution to the problem
5. Send a thank you note and apologize again
6. Do not make the SAME mistake again

Ninety-nine percent of the time, this procedure will get a happier customer than if you had been perfect the first time. This is "Blameless Problem Solving." In a nutshell, apologize for the problem, do not blame anyone, fix it quickly and learn from the situation.

When our oldest customer is asked for a referral, he says, "Tovar is not perfect, they make mistakes, but when they do they own up to it, fix it quickly and take it off the plate."

Our mistakes and those of others can be our greatest teachers.

Most successful people have made many mistakes over their lifetime. Life is an amazing, sometimes unpredictable learning experience (if you embrace it that way). Each day when we awaken, stretch toward the heavens and put one foot in front of the other. Our own reality show is usually right there waiting for us to give our attention to whatever situations, dealing and coping with issues, surprises, laughter, and we make decisions based on what we know at the time. We could live in a bubble and say we are playing it safe. The question becomes, why are we not *living in the front section, but choosing to hang out* in the nosebleed seats. For those of us, who want to find our life purpose, live it and set goals, we know instinctively we must experience life from the front section. It can be scary sometimes but....

As the French say, "*bon courage.*" It takes courage, to live and to step out of your comfort zones and experience life and its unknowns.

Mistakes happen. They are our custom-made learning tools, as painful as some mistakes may be. Our biggest mistakes are refusing to learn from our mistakes, and failing to take responsibility for them. Rather than walk through the moment the mistakes bring too many of us shut down with feelings of shame and fear of failure.

Know what two iconic men had to say about failure? "Failure is simply the opportunity to begin again more intelligently," said Henry Ford. Thomas Edison said, "I have not failed. I now know 10,000 ways that won't work."

Work with a Sense of Urgency While Being Relentless About Continuous Improvement

> "If I asked people what they wanted they
> would have told me faster horses."
>
> — *Henry Ford*

TOVAR WAY FUNDAMENTAL: WORK WITH A SENSE OF URGENCY

In today's world, people expect everything in a nano-second. As snow fighters, we must continually work with a sense of urgency.

You probably don't remember the days when you made a phone call and if no one answered, you would just have to keep calling back until they did answer. That problem led to the invention of answering machines making it possible to leave messages. Then came pagers, fax machines, cell phones, text messaging and, of course email and social media. Now with ripe innovations we may have to consider a chip in our heads and telepathy as the next big tools for communicating.

The world keeps moving faster and faster and people expect immediate responses.

Be of the mindset that 'time waits for no one.' Work with a sense of urgency to get things done. Here are some thoughts on how to do that:

1. *Seize* the opportunity.
2. Learn to identify key information necessary for smart decision-making.
3. Gather the facts
4. Evaluate the options thoroughly
5. Make a decision
6. Get moving

Do not fall into a slacker mentality. Thoroughness and decisiveness are not mutually exclusive. Be action-oriented. In other words, make a decision and get moving. I have seen too many people overthink something and never get moving.

What does urgency mean? It means performing tasks quickly with excellent results. To the customer it means quick, efficient service with minimal hassle, great attitude and getting onto the next situation. To our company it means being efficient in order to compete on a high level in the world market and do what all businesses want: deliver the best product with the best price at the best profit so we can have happier employees and shareholders.

What does work with a sense of urgency really mean? I am not talking about creating an environment where people feel anxious and buzz around like bumblebees on steroids. What I am saying is having the resolve and inclination to take action: boldly and quickly. There *is* a difference between being patient and being a procrastinator. Procrastination is the act of non-action in order to avoid taking action (on something). Having patience on the other hand, involves acts of strategic action within the flow of things.

Joe Caruso is TSP's longest customer. He is a successful businessman, father and husband. The proof is in his children who are all grown and successful in their own right.

Joe and his wife are 'Snowbirds' that envied group of Chicagoans who flock to Florida for four months during the winter, each year. You know what Joe once told me and I never forgot?

He said, "The more problems you can solve for people the more money you can make."

As I said before, I did not come from a privileged background. I was born Midwest middle class. I came from an average home with extraordinary, positive parents. Lucky break #1. We were not in the top 2, 10, 20, 50 or even 75% of income earners. Now we had everything we needed: shelter, food, water, education, opportunity, love and oh yes, oxygen.

What I did as a kid was not rocket science. I was paid to cut lawns for neighbors. I was paid to solve problems for them. Eventually, I was cutting 100 lawns. I hustled. Then I hired people to help and taught them how I mowed each lawn. Then I hustled some more. The more lawns we cut, the more problems we were solving for customers.

The main problem our customers had was that the world is a very busy place; people had work obligations, family obligations and kids who took up lots of time on their lists of things to do. No surprises there. So for a reasonable price, people paid me to give them two or three hours or more back on the weekend. My services solved a piece of a problem: people have so little time to do so many things on their lists. They could depend on me to take care of their lawns. Done.

In reading a *Pick the Brain* post inspired by *The Magic of Thinking Big* by David J. Schwartz, *"Despite the simplicity of this concept (of getting things done), there is a perpetual shortage of people who excel at getting results…People at the top of every profession share one quality—they get things done. This ability supersedes intelligence, talent and connections in determining the size of one's salary and the speed of one's advancement."*

My 22-year-old nephew recently started a business that makes house calls for detailing cars, motorcycles and boats. He has "the hustle" in his DNA. He charges a fee competitive with a car wash and gets a task done with a sense of urgency.

What has he done? Because detailing takes time, he solves the problem of taking their car to the car wash to be detailed, having to have someone pick them up and bring them back or sit and wait. He gives his customer the option of using their time to do other things. The only way he can make good money is to detail the vehicle(s) quickly, efficiently and do a great job so he generates referrals: the best kind of business.

Would you believe he details 1000's of vehicles each spring, summer and fall in the Chicago area? There he is at 22 years old 'problem-solver' on his way to building a successful business. He hustles.

This, I know for sure, you do not have to be a rocket scientist to have success (positive results) in business and in life.

TOVAR WAY FUNDAMENTAL: BE RELENTLESS ABOUT CONTINUOUS IMPROVEMENT

Constantly evaluate everything you do. Do not be satisfied with the status quo. The most successful people and organizations are in a never-ending pursuit of improvement.

I am a life-long learner, a student of the world. Henry Ford said, "Anyone who stops learning is old, whether at twenty or eighty."

You work for "You Incorporated" and when you work with a sense of urgency, you create a *brand* of reliability that schools, employers, and the public want. The *brand*? That brand is, 'I want it now." Deliver it now and you are on your way to massive success. No matter if, you are a student, an employee, a doctor, lawyer, business owner, etc. YOU work for you and are in business for yourself.

I personally spend thousands of dollars each year for my continuing education, whether through executive coaches, classes, seminars and/or conferences. At TSP, we spend thousands of dollars on our employees training, enrichment and continuing education. Learning is how we continuously improve.

Relentless, the dictionary defines this word as ceaseless and intense and persistently hostile…in pursuit, can't stop now kind of attitude. It is okay to be satisfied with the status quo, the way things are now, how they currently exist. The difference between the passions eluded by someone who is "relentless" versus one who is satisfied, speaks volumes about the level a person wants to live their life and play the game.

I have a little story about legendary golfer Arnold Palmer, a dead-on example of the old golfer adage, 'drive for show; putt for dough.' At a driving range, Palmer, 80, was seen tapping the same putt repeatedly for almost three hours. A man watching him asked, "How can you do this, hitting the same putt over and over again for hours and aren't you bored to death? I would be." Arnold Palmer responded,"…what level do you want to play the game? It all depends on what level you want to play the game." Relentless continuous improvement usually takes practice. So what are you willing to do? *Celebrity Net Worth* lists Arnold Palmer as the third wealthiest American athlete at $675 million, beating out Michael Jordan.

When you have a thirst to learn and want to be the best at what you do, no one has to force you. However, it does take persistence. That's why my favorite quote is about persistence from Calvin Coolidge:

"Nothing in this world can take the place of persistence. Talent will not; nothing is more common than unsuccessful people with talent. Genius will not; unrewarded genius is almost a proverb. Education will not; the world is full of educated failures. Persistence and determination alone are omnipotent."

To be omnipotent or have great power and authority is not a bad place to live. However, it is essential that you know what you know and what you don't know. Knowing what you don't know, having an open-mind (everyone isn't like you or think like you and vice versa) and learning from those who have been there is how many successful people have done it.

Being open to continuous improvement makes some people uneasy because it forces a person to look at what may need fixing. Samuel Granados, President of Integrated Resource Systems puts it like this, *"I have found the real unequivocal meaning of success is through hardship. It is hard to be open; being open makes many people feel vulnerable and uncomfortable. If you have a vision for yourself, as I have/had I find you have to strive for excellence in everything you choose to do and strive with joy even when it is hard/painful/difficult. Some hardships breed more wisdom and knowledge than others do. Transformation and improvement through hardship hold the (golden) key to life. I find it amazing how such simple usually painful occurrences can lead to such extraordinary successes. Some of Jeff and mine most memorable failures/hardships have led to our most formidable victories and accomplishments."*

Damn near everything you may say or try has been done before. Reach out and connect to people to mentor you through a situation or on a general basis.

Be proud to be a student of life. "When the student is ready, the teacher will appear."

— *Buddhist proverb*

When you seek out continuous improvement, you cannot operate in a silo to improve. When you ask and associate with the right people, pay attention. You have landed in an environment to learn, listen and implement.

In our mission statement, we talk about continuous improvement. There are of course a million ways to improve. I want to share some ways that have worked for me.

Mentors: I found that successful people love to share what they did and tell their story if only they are asked. Now you may have to ask five people before one will be willing to share (I have found 90% are willing to help but not all and that's ok). But, it matters who you ask and how you ask. When I was creating the snow only business, I watched and learned from my local competition. I was seen as a threat and rightly so. Therefore, I went to our national association and found guys from Minneapolis, Cincinnati, Pennsylvania, Cleveland, Connecticut and New Jersey and more who would share every detail of how they did it if I asked. Asking is a powerful tool. Ask, receive, say thank you and send a written thank you note with a small gift. The world opens up to you. The world becomes yours.

Formal education: this is not necessary but it does open doors. I went through college, then graduate school to get an MBA and will someday go back and earn a doctorate degree. Education is fun for me. I enjoy being in an environment of learning energy. However, if education is not fun for you, then go back to number 1—Mentors. I found a dozen great teachers who became mentors to me: a few in high school but most in college.

Read, watch movies, documentaries, informational TV, listen to music, audio books. Find a way that fits for you to learn and improve what you are doing. The key thing for my nephew in his car detail business will be to continue to evolve to get better. Charles Darwin said, "It is not the strongest of species that survives, but the most adaptable." Never stop learning, changing and be on a relentless search for continuous improvement.

Hannibal once said, "We will find our way or make one." For me, that is the key to life; find a way or make a way. Nothing is impossible. Many things are said to be impossible. In fact, I heard years ago that the head of the United States Patent Office said, "Everything that can be invented has been invented." Now I don't know if this is true, but most of us now know that inventions and new technology will never end.

My point is there are many ways to learn and improve. There is no one-way. Find the way that works for you. Live with a relentless, persistent sense of urgency to accomplish continuous improvement.

Honor Commitments and Take Responsibility for Achieving Results

"I have a loyalty that runs in my bloodstream, when I lock into someone or something, you can't get me away from it because I commit that thoroughly. That's in friendship, that's in a deal, that's a commitment. Don't give me paper—I can get the same lawyer who drew it up to break it. But if you shake my hand, that's for life."

— Jerry Lewis

Your word—in the end is all you have. When you give your word, it is your bond. Now, *no one* is perfect, but when it comes to giving your word to someone, that merits near perfection.

Once you break your word, it becomes easier to break it a second time, a third time, and so forth. We have all broken our word for one reason or another with someone or even ourselves. Once you start, it becomes easier to tell a lie. Repetition of any habit makes it easier to repeat. Therefore, I choose to reinforce good habits in my life instead of bad ones.

When you keep your word, people know they can count on you to do what you say you're going to do. You know what else? *You know* deep down that *you* can count on *yourself*.

When you are building a team, it is important to look for others who have the same fundamental value; when they give their word, it means something to them. Life is really about the people who surround you. Surround yourself with honorable people and when they tell you something will be done—it will.

TOVAR WAY FUNDAMENTAL: HONOR COMMITMENTS

Providing heroic customer service involves a complex chain of interdependent activities. People count on us and we count on each other to do our part in this chain. Honoring our commitments make the chain unbreakable. Do what you say you are going to do, when you say you are going to do it. If a commitment cannot be fulfilled, notify others early and agree upon a new commitment. There are times when things change and a commitment cannot be kept: like when a flight is cancelled. We know that scenario far too well living here in Chicagoland, especially when it comes to inclement weather. How do you handle this? When this happens, you must contact the person with whom you made the commitment and explain the situation. Make a new commitment to honor the previous one even if it means driving instead of flying the next time in order to get there.

I remember a situation where we had to honor a commitment that we would lose significant money on. The mistake was ours. We honored the commitment but realized there had to be a better way to do that job. This commitment was a large landscape contract on a water treatment plant, which we refer to as a 'B property' but even the B property had to look good and we had underestimated our costs. We brought in a consultant who showed us new methods and equipment to use to produce exceptional results on our jobs. In the end, that job became one of our best producing jobs. The interesting thing is after that mistake, we built our company around only jobs that we could give our customers a great price, great service (as they defined it) and we made higher margins. If not for a mistake and our positive, proactive approach to correct the mistake, we would have never learned a better way to do that kind of job.

Mistakes often make the way to a better way.

A friend, who owns a box-making company, got a big new account and then entered into a contract to buy a larger facility. The bank was going to give him a loan based on the contract. He had a great deal pending on the facility purchase and then, the big new account pulled out. Then the bank pulled out. Think he crashed and burned? Just the opposite. To honor his commitment, he created a solution by selling his contract for the building to a real estate company with a guarantee to lease back the building for 10 years. Therefore, by using a smart, positive approach, my friend made $2M with a single deal, got his building, made and sold a lot of boxes and shortly thereafter landed another big new contract.

I asked him how he came up with the solution. He said, "When you're screwed, you find a way to make something happen."

Why wait until you're screwed? Because sometimes it takes situations that slam us against a wall and force us to dig deeper, push harder or greater than ever before. Maybe it is the notion that when things are at a breaking point you have nothing to lose. My advice? Divert drama whenever possible and keep a positive frame of mind to make things happen.

TOVAR WAY FUNDAMENTAL: TAKE RESPONSIBILITY FOR ACHIEVING RESULTS

While we appreciate effort, we reward and celebrate results. Excuses do not get the job done. Embrace numbers and accountability. Metrics help us understand how we are doing and how we can improve on our performance. Hold yourself accountable for achieving results.

Results often mean looking at performance and numbers. For me, I try to keep it simple. I don't need 100 metrics to keep my business on track. I keep it down to this: profit, cash flow, controlling overhead, gross margin, sales results, customer and employee (evaluations). This may be different from some other leaders however; this is what works for me.

As Jeff Bladt and Bob Filbin explain in HBR Blog Network (Harvard Business Review), "Communication is an essential ingredient in how data is collected and thus, interpreted. Are you focusing on the wrong metric? There is a difference between numbers and numbers that matter. There is a difference between vanity metrics and meaningful metrics. Do not approach a situation as with a 'one size fits all' perspective. It is crucial to factor in your knowledge of the individual situation and/or client when you do your due diligence— research and analysis—to confirm salient facts."

In the end when it comes to achieving results, profitability drives all the other numbers that bankers and accountants want to see generated. There are various ratios they consider, and their numbers reveal a lot. If you keep your eyes on the Profit & Loss statement, the accountants can run all the other numbers and explain them to you once or twice a year.

Each year at our company, I offer to facilitate a book club where we read Jack Canfield's, "Success Principles." His book has 64 principles that I believe, (if you can incorporate 8-10 into your life), are stepping-stones to great success. In one of the first chapters, Jack talks about taking complete responsibility. Every year this really resonates with people as we talk about how important it is and how often we don't take complete responsibility for our results. We often make excuses or blame others, but these are just time and energy wasters that do not get anyone closer to their desired outcome.

Is it possible to take complete responsibility or are there times when we need to use that defense mechanism not to have it fall all on us? We talk about teamwork but when a part of the team blows it, it seems easy to pass the blame to them.

I remember many years ago when the Chicago Bears had a great defense but not so great of an offense. The defense would make fun of the offense, side stepped their own responsibility and the Bears lost several games. Then a new sheriff came to town, Mike Ditka. The funny thing was that Ditka inherited Buddy Ryan, a defensive coach, who he could not fire.

Mike decided rather than complain he would take complete responsibility for the results. When he did, the Bears began to win. The defense gave up few points and they scored. They took responsibility, and then the special teams started to score. Then the offense started to score. It was not until they 'owned it' by taking responsibility that the Bears won.

I mention this because even when you are part of a team, it matters what you do on and off the field, in our case in and outside of the workplace. When you play the blame game, not much productivity happens. When you help the team rise up and do more than your part, you begin to win as a team.

The point is it is our responsibility to choose our attitude and our actions, as well as how we look at our job and our life.

There are 168 hours per week. Out of those 168 hours, I work, sleep and do life-stuff. For the majority of those hours, I love what I do and I have fun doing it. I read something in the *New York Times* that Brad Smith, CEO of Intuit, a $3 billion software company said, that resonated with me. He was talking about leadership when he taught an entire martial arts school, "At that point, you know nothing, your journey begins. At the same time, you are measured on the progress of the students you're teaching. It's no longer about your own abilities; it's about building the capacity in others. I fall back on that to this day, realizing there's a lot to learn, and also recognizing that success is creating the environment where people can be their best selves and continue to grow and develop...I tell people: Do what you love...."

As the leader, I do whatever it takes to learn more and set the standard for honoring commitments and taking responsibility for achieving results. A practice, I would not ask my people to do unless I did it myself. Should-have-would-have-could-have—are not part of honoring commitments or respecting what you love. As George Washington Carver put it, "99% of failures come from people who have the habit of making excuses."

For my daughters, I really keep it simple. They want to participate in sports and other afterschool activities—then their responsibility is to keep their grades at A or B levels. I know—without a doubt— with minimal amounts of efforts, they can achieve that.

When we learn to take responsibility, excuses are not needed. There will always be a reason why something didn't happen. The only reasons that matter are the ones we take away from the experience so we don't fail the next time.

My girls do not say, "That's not fair" anymore. Because every time they would say something was not fair, I would say, "You are right, life is not fair and you're lucky it is not. If life were fair, you might have had to live in an orphanage in Africa without sufficient water, food, education and healthcare." The reason I mention the orphanages in Africa is that an employee and his wife have adopted six children from orphanages in Africa. From what I've learned first-hand from them is there are thousands of children who live in Third World countries—like Africa—who would never have the chance of living a life like the one we have in the United States. My employee's kids came to America and are thankful for every opportunity America has to offer. Many people, who are born here, take this country for granted and become weighted-down by flaws instead of motivated by available opportunities.

Who is responsible for your happiness? Own it. No one can make anyone happy; although there can be outside factors, we are responsible for our own happiness.

Bill Boggs has many words of wisdom to pass on that relate to taking responsibility for our achievements. Bill simply says, "Study the greats." In other words, draw wisdom from those who have been there, done that. Why reinvent the wheel when you do not have to.

Here's a slice of what Bill has to say in his own words. "When I interviewed Frank Sinatra on my TV show, 'Midday Live with Bill Boggs', Sinatra spoke of the impact Tommy Dorsey, the great trombonist and bandleader, had on his life. Frank loved Dorsey's long-note breathing technique, which he said, "could leave you feeling breathless." Dorsey eventually became Sinatra's mentor and influenced his life in many ways.

Frank Sinatra had a huge influence on me in many ways. Probably the most important of which was his suggestions that I study great people, I was interviewing on television: to explore the reasons behind their success. Since Frank, I've interviewed thousands of people—presidents, business moguls, global leaders, and sports' stars, heroes from the daily news, artists, actors, singers and beyond. I applied Frank's suggestion to explore the powers that enable great success."

He continues, "Exploring the powers that enable great success in someone can help to empower your own actions and drive you to greater heights.

I wrote an entire book based on that premise. I conducted a series of interviews with winners like Sir Richard Branson, Dr. Mehmet Oz, Diane von Furstenberg, Donald Trump, Joe Torre, Clive Davis and many more. My aim with that book, "Got What it Takes?" was to tap into the "experienced wisdom" of people who'd reached the top in their profession. By becoming a student of successful people, you create your mentors and role models. In the process you lay out your own road map to success."

A great attitude can take you a long way in this world. Every day you get up, you have a choice; make it a great day or don't. Take responsibility.

As Abe Lincoln said, "Most people are as happy as they make up their minds to be."

Success leaves clues...

Mentor (noun)

"wise advisor," 1750,
from Greek Mentor, a friend of Odysseus and advisor
of the young Telemachus in the Homer's *Odyssey*

The name appears to be an agent noun of mentos, "intent, purpose, spirit, passion."

- Socrates mentored Plato
- Hayden mentored Beethoven
- Freud mentored Jung
- Oprah Winfrey mentored by Mrs. Duncan (4th grade teacher) and Maya Angelou
- Starbuck's Howard Schultz mentored by Warren Bennis
- General Colin Powell mentored by his father, Luther Powell
- Charles Schwab (1st president of US Steel) mentored by Andrew Carnegie
- Star War's Luke Skywalker mentored by Yoda and Obi-Wan-Ben Kenobi
- Henry David Thoreau mentored by Ralph Waldo Emerson
- Steve Jobs mentored Larry Page from Google
- Sir Freddie Laker, founder of Laker Airways mentored Richard Branson, Virgin Airlines

MENTOR

Taking responsibility comes forth in how one approaches their life and their job. Jon Gordon talks about the difference between *"I have to take care of this customer versus I get to take care of this customer"* attitude. He writes, *"I get to do a job when so many are (out of work). We get to interact with employees and customers and make a difference in their life. We get to use our gifts and talents to make a product or provide a service."*

JON GORDON,
BEST SELLING AUTHOR,
THE JON GORDON COMPANIES

MENTOR

I always preached about the importance of knowing WHERE you make your money in business and to focus on those areas.

Jeff was a sponge and I really admire that. So many people listen to mentors, speakers and advisors and then continue to do the same old same old. He really listened to his mentors and those who were further up the learning curve than he was. He took the best of the best advice and achieved incredible success.

DAVID MINOR
CHAIRMAN & CEO, THE LANDSCAPE PARTNERS
FOUNDER EMERITUS: THE NEELEY ENTREPREUNERSHIP CENTER AT TCU
TEXAS CHRISTIAN UNIVERSITY IN DALLAS

Mentor

Our relationship started off because as two owners of snow plow businesses, we had a lot in common. We have been friends for 14 years. It began with a mastermind group of snow fighters that Jeff founded. When together, we swap stories, thoughts, ideas, share best practices, business plans and the little known stuff like what type of shovels do you use or what do you look for when you hire.

To mentor is to be in an intimate advisory position. My advice is:

- To have love and passion for life
- Live life with purpose

I have a deep desire to understand the truth: how things work, why did that happen? What can someone do to help that person?

I take self-inventory all the time. I ask myself, 'what did I do to help? Interspection of myself about three times per day of how I handle problems and how I perceive things.

Our business requires quick and accurate decisions. When we 'man our battle stations' in the as a snow fighter, every event has elements of Murphy's Law on steroids. People look to us for safety and comfort in a whirlwind of crisis.

But the thing that measured a man for me was when Jeff said he had long forgiven the men whose actions resulted in his father's paralysis.

NORM DETRICK
OWNER, RELIABLE SNOW PLOWING SPECIALISTS

Mentor

A good mentoring situation must have a high degree of trust and credibility going both ways. Then the mentor gains trust by listening as much as telling. And it is in the listening where the mentor many times can become the mentee, applying things the student says to even gain a deeper understanding of the things he is teaching.

JIM PALUCH
PRESIDENT, JP HORIZONS
AUTHOR

Mentor

"Developing a vision and then figuring out a model and structure to operate grow and replicate your business is the ultimate. Jeff always hung onto the concept and has honed it to the highest level in his company. Having snow branches with management structured effectively is a feat, very few can say they've achieved this in their company. Critical if you desire growth and want to maintain competency on a larger scale. "

MIKE RORIE
CEO, GIS DYNAMICS

Mentor

I first met Jeff in the mid-nineties. He had invited me into his company to advise him and his management team in the art of financial management. In those days, he was working out of a dilapidated hut—he and seven other persons in a space not fit for four.

The condition of the company was fairly typical of the chaos one might expect of a start-up with one big exception—Jeff Tovar.

Jeff manages with a unique combination of tenacity and repetition. He reminds me of a gunny sergeant I had long ago—practice, practice, practice until we get it right—then repeat, repeat, repeat.

There is a passion in his belly that I recognized early on. This guy is good, I thought—he is going places—and, boy, will he be fun to watch!

From a peanut operation in Elgin, Illinois to a global force in the snow management industry, Jeff has indeed been fun to watch – and, he is not finished yet!

FRANK H ROSS
ROSS-PAYNE & ASSOCIATES, INC.

Epilogue

"You are not alone."

— *Michael Jackson*

Y ou have read it before especially in this book but it cannot be said enough, "There are very few situations in life that have never occurred before. It is why the age-old statement 'history repeats itself' still remains relevant even today. When you find yourself feeling stuck, needing help/wisdom or a fresh perspective ask someone who has accomplishments similar to ones you want to achieve if they would share how they made it to the top. Before you contact them, do your homework, approach mentors with humility and respect for their time and advice. During the time you have with them, LISTEN and not be distracted with anticipation and/or expectations: listen and follow through. Do not forget to say thank you anc send a thank you note.

My Mentors:

BILL BOGGS

Four-time Emmy Award winning Television interviewer and professional speaker

www.billboggs.com
www.billboggsspeaks.com
Billboggstv on YouTube
"Got What it Takes"

JOE CARUSO

Semi-retired Business Owner
Real estate investor

GISELLE CHAPMAN

President & Chief Performance Optimizer

Chapman Business Solutions, Inc.

www.gisellechapman.com

JOHN G. CHIARELLA, JR.

President

Ultimate Professional Grounds
Management

www.ultimategrounds.com

NORM DETRICK

President

Reliable Snowplowing

www.Reliablesnowplowing.net

DAVID J. FRIEDMAN

Author, Speaker, Consultant

www.djfriedman.com

STEVE FUZINSKI

Owner,

Green Sweep, Inc.

www.greensweepinc.com

JON GORDON

**Best-selling Author, Business Consultant
& Keynote Speaker**

www.jongordon.com

SAMUEL GRANADOS

President,

Integrated Resource Systems, Inc.

www.integratedsnow.com

DAVID MINOR

The Landscape Partners

www.thelandscapepartners.com
"Never put business before your family."

MARK MOORE

Owner & Vice President

Winter Services, Inc.
www.winterservices.net

JIM PALUCH

President and Author,

JP Horizons Incorporated

www.jphorizons.com

BERNARD E. ROLLIN, PHD.

University Distinguished Professor of Philosophy, Animal Sciences & Biomedical Sciences

www.colostate.edu

MIKE RORIE

CEO
GIS Dynamics

www.gisdynamics.com

FRANK H ROSS

Ross-Payne & Associates, Inc.

DENNIS TOVAR and SHARON TOVAR

Jeff's Father & Mother

≈ In Memoriam ≈

Dr. Pexton was my college advisor and professor for a number of classes. However, as I look back he was so much more than the advisors of any of my friends.

This man guided his students and helped them find their way. He required all of his freshman to take a class with him on how to study and succeed in college.

He then required all his seniors to take a class with him on how to succeed outside of college. He challenged me to write my first business plan and to create a business that had nothing to do with what he taught (animal science).

Further, he first introduced me to many of the skills talked about in this book. At the time, we often do not realize the value of the gifts given to us by a man like Dr. Pexton. Looking back, I now realize I truly was blessed to have this great man in my life.

For over 23 years, Jeff Tovar has built Tovar Snow Professionals from a handful of lawnmowers to the largest minority-owned snow-only company in the United States. He has accomplished this through fearlessly embracing continuous improvement, innovation and heroic customer service with like-minded heroes (employees).

Jeff's roots stem from an immigrant grandfather born in Mexico City who wanted a better life for his children and grandchildren. Entrepreneurial as a child, Tovar began the business during his high school years. He is a graduate of Colorado State University, and the proceeded to earn his MBA at Lake Forest Graduate School of Management.

Tovar has developed many relationships over the years on the executive level with customers, corporate partners and within the minority community. He prides himself on "doing the right thing" along with the "Tovar Way" and has developed a company culture to live by these values.

As a Certified Snow Professional, he serves as a board member of the Chicago Minority Supplier Development Council, and is an active member of the Illinois Hispanic Chamber of Commerce. Jeff was founder and past president of the International Snow & Ice Management Association (SIMA). Tovar is also a proud member of the International Facility Management Association (IFMA), Building Owners Management Association (BOMA), American Public Works Association (APWA), International Council of Shopping Centers (ICSC) and Planet Landcare Network. He has had the honor to nationally speak for many of these associations along with publications in *Snow & Ice Magazine, Lawn & Landscape, Negocios Now* and the 2013 edition of the *Chicago Minority Business Report*.

Maintaining an "attitude of servitude," Tovar has created "Snow Angels" (formerly "Tovar Cares") in which he and his employees volunteer for and donate to many charitable organizations such as American Cancer Society, Relay for Life, Goodwill Industries, Life Source, United Way, Ronald McDonald House and Little Angels to name a few.

Tovar Snow Professionals brings value by providing Instant Communication, Instant Action and Instant Relaxation for snow and ice management services. Tovar has implemented operations and customer communication procedures that allows effective service during the worst conditions. They immediately respond to any issues that may arise allowing customers to enjoy a stress-free winter.